MW01174587

COMMON VALOR

GENERAL AREA OF DIVISION OPERATIONS

MAP SUPPLIED BY FIRST DIVISION MUSEUM, WHEATON, ILLINOIS.

Common Valor

★ ★ ★ ★ ★

Ambush at Srok Rung
November 7, 1967

By

S. T. SIMMS

Foreword by

PAUL F. GORMAN
General, U.S. Army (Retired)

LITTLE MIAMI PUBLISHING CO.
Milford, Ohio
2010

Little Miami Publishing Co.
P.O. Box 588
Milford, Ohio 45150-0588
www.littlemiamibooks.com

Copyright ©2010 by S. T. Simms. All rights reserved. No part of this book may be reproduced or transmitted in any form or by any means, electronic or mechanical, including photocopying, recording or by any information storage and retrieval system without written permission from the author, except for the inclusion of brief quotations in a review.

Third printing 2012

Printed in the United States of America on acid-free paper.

ISBN-13: 978-1-932250-81-7
ISBN-10: 1-932250-81-6

Library of Congress Control Number: 2010925431

Dedication

The American infantryman makes the offer of his life when he takes up his rifle and assumes his place in the ranks because, by standing with his comrades, he puts his life on the line for their collective success. From some, payment of that offered sacrifice is required. For others the payment is waived: and having survived by God's good grace, they return home carrying the memories of those who died and bearing the obligation to make our country worthy of their sacrifice.

BLUE SPADER MAJ. THOMAS GALVIN (RETIRED)

This book is dedicated to all who served our country in the Vietnam conflict. Regardless of what has been written and said about the war, communism remains at its core a godless and oppressive political ideology. It stands as the antithesis of the self-evident truth "that all men are endowed by their creator with certain unalienable rights, that among these are life, liberty, and the pursuit of happiness." To fight against those who would use any means to take the lives, liberty and pursuit of happiness from others must always remain a noble undertaking. The aftermath of our departure from Indochina has proven the worthiness of our cause. The blood of the innocent multitudes that died in Vietnam, Cambodia, and Laos after we left is on the hands of our fellow citizens who opposed the war and reviled our military at every turn. And for our heroes that sacrificed their lives, may God have mercy upon their souls and bless those they left behind.

Contents

Foreword

THE 26TH INFANTRY REGIMENT has earned a prominent place in the proud history of the 1st Infantry Division of the United States Army. The 26th's regimental color, its flag, is decorated with streamers signifying award of a Presidential Unit Citation, a victory at Stolberg, Germany, and a Valorous Unit Award for its triumph at Ap Gu, Vietnam. That color bears other symbols of recognition for heroic accomplishment by France, Belgium, and the Republic of Vietnam. Among the three battalions that once comprised the regiment, the 1st Battalion stands out for its deeds in World Wars I and II and in Vietnam; in the latter conflict, after Army restructuring had eliminated the 2d and 3d battalions, it served alone. Part of the prowess of the Blue Spaders—a sobriquet for the 26th Infantry stemming from the blue arrowhead on the uniform badge of its soldiers—rests upon determination to live up to the deeds of those who had served before them.

Yet the 26th Infantry has known the bitterness of defeat as well as the ebullience of victory; indeed, battle losses have seemed to add to its resilience. In 1943, in the throat of the Kasserine Pass, it was torn asunder by Erwin Rommel's Afrika Korps, and in 1944 it lost entire rifle companies at Stolberg and in the Hürtgen Forest. Despite these setbacks, the 26th Infantry thereafter went forward the more firmly resolved to prevail against the Germans, and in 1944 it defended resolutely the northern shoulder of the Bulge, and in 1945 it drove relentlessly across Germany and into Czechoslovakia.

In November 1967, the 272d Regiment of the 9th VC Division—a nominally Viet Cong (southern communist) formation—successfully ambushed 1st Battalion, 26th Infantry. This vivid account of that action has been written by a veteran who was there, drawing on the experience of fellow Blue Spaders.

The undersigned knew the 272d Regiment well, having fought against it in 1966 and early 1967 when its members wore black pajama-like peasant garb. I walked the position of 1st Battalion, 26th Infantry at Ap Gu, and I know from the interrogation of an enemy officer that the 272d, following that crushing repulse, had withdrawn to Cambodia, where its depleted ranks were filled with North Vietnamese replacements, and it was rearmed and retrained in preparation for an offensive in early 1968. That training stressed the importance of tactics of decapitation that concentrated fires around American radio antennae, and of using plunging fire against Americans, who reacted to surprise by assuming a prone firing position vulnerable to attack from above.

The battles around Loc Ninh in late 1967 were calculated rehearsals for the Tet Offensive of February 1968: the 272d, then outfitted in green North Vietnamese uniforms, was sent across the border of Cambodia to employ their new weapons, and to put into practice their newly learned tactics. The engagement described here probably gratified their North Vietnamese commanders, but at its end the Blue Spaders controlled the battlefield, recovered their wounded and dead, and went on to regain battle readiness, taught by their experience at Srok Rung to be newly wary of a more capable foe.

The reader should note that 1st Battalion, 26th Infantry, continues to serve the United States, and that in Iraq, in 2006 it was posted in the Adhamiyah neighborhood of Baghdad, the most notoriously violent precinct in that violent capital, and there sustained unprecedented casualties. It was Company C that bore the brunt of the actions at Stolberg, again at Ap Gu and Srok Rung, and once more at Adhamiyah. 1-26 Infantry, deployed in Iraq for fifteen months, suffered fourteen KIA and twenty-two WIA, more losses in one battalion than in any other, in any division, since Vietnam. The 1st Division's motto is a tribute to such a unit:

No Mission Too Difficult, No Sacrifice Too Great, Duty First

Paul F. Gorman
General, U.S. Army (Retired)

Preface

MILITARY BATTLES COMMAND A VERY NARROW RANGE OF INTEREST, yet they deserve to be chronicled for the sake of history. The battle of Loc Ninh (October 29–November 7, 1967) comprises a key piece of the Vietnam War story, especially because of its relationship to the Communist Tet Offensive of January 1968. The ambush at Srok Rung on November 7 was a part of the Loc Ninh fighting and, since no one else has written an in-depth account of the battle, the responsibility has fallen upon me.

Like chess games, military battles entail many possible moves. Those moves can be reviewed, analyzed, and critiqued. But unlike chess games where players can see all the pieces, military battles are often fought against invisible foes. The decisions that are made prior to and in the heat of the conflict must be reviewed, present and future, and learned from by interested parties and combat leaders.

On November 7, enemy soldiers showed themselves and fled before an advancing First Infantry Division combat patrol, disappearing into the jungle straight ahead. Many suspected an ambush. A critical decision had to be made: pursue the fleeing enemy, turn from the area of suspected danger, or rake the area with artillery fire and then proceed with either of the first two options. Each decision would yield a different outcome. The choice made that day is forever stamped in stone, but with the perspective of hindsight the "what ifs?" engendered remain. The battle that ensued is here recounted through the eyes of many that fought there on that day and is told from many different perspectives. Particularly noteworthy are the many acts of valor evident in the commentaries of the surviving combatants that I interviewed.

Another motive for this book is because some of the families of those who died there want to know. Hopefully, it will answer questions long gone unanswered and bring some closure even after all these years.

In telling the story of the battle of November 7, I have sought to interview as many of the participants as possible. I'm not sure that the story could have been told much earlier than the present time, now some forty years after it took place. Certainly without an active 26th Infantry Regiment Association and its outreach efforts in the late 1990s to recruit members from the Vietnam era through the present time, it would have been very difficult for me to locate as many of the eye-witnesses as have been found. Also, it seems that it took a considerable passage of time before many of the battle's survivors were able to talk about the experience. The impact of the trauma of that day left many without any desire to dredge up emotions that had been suppressed for many years. The bonds that develop among soldiers living together and facing danger 24/7 can be strong and enduring. Loss can be devastating. One of the key contributors declined a number of requests for an interview and agreed to talk with me about November 7 only after being persuaded by one of his former platoon members who accompanied me on the trip to his home. A number of individuals that I was able to contact were not willing to talk about that day at all and would not participate in the project.

Of course there remain some inconsistencies in time and location; I have done my best to resolve these. The stories of several of those interviewed have been edited for the sake of clarity and readability. Many of the Blue Spader's observations regarding the initial moments of the battle are repetitive, but have been included so that the reader can more fully understand the perspective of individual soldiers in different locations at that critical time of the battle. All interviews were personally conducted by the author either face to face or over the telephone. From the beginning my goal has been to be as historically accurate as possible. Events are not necessarily in chronological sequence within each chapter, although that was my intent in piecing together the individual stories.

S. T. Simms

Acknowledgments

THE ENCOURAGEMENT AND ASSISTANCE OF GEN. PAUL GORMAN, a former 26th Regiment Battalion commander, was invaluable to this project from start to finish. Paul provided me with reference books and maps and even gave me the blood-stained, bullet and shrapnel riddled map that Charlie Company Commander Len Tavernetti carried in the battle of November 7 (the map now resides in the 1st Division Archives in Wheaton, Illinois). It is a portion of this restored map which appears on the front cover. Seeing Paul every year at the annual Blue Spader reunions and his availability for consultation by telephone and e-mail kept me going over the past nine years even when motivation was flagging.

I owe thanks to John Votaw, Ph.D., the former director of the First Division Museum and Research Center in Wheaton, Illinois. John was instrumental in getting the interviewing process started by providing recording and videotape equipment for the initial series of interviews conducted at the Blue Spader reunion in New Orleans in 2002. Special thanks is due to Paul Herbert, who took over as director upon John's retirement. Paul was especially helpful in the final stages getting ready for publication. Credit is due also to the staff at the Research Center—Andrew Woods, Eric Gillespie, and Steve Hawkins—for their aid in utilizing the Research Center archives.

I benefitted significantly from the assistance of Maj. Tom Galvin (Blue Spader, June–August 1966 and January–December 1969). Tom was always willing to help in any way that he could, which included searches at the National Archives near his home.

I owe a major debt to fellow veteran Jim Charland whose tireless efforts at locating former Blue Spaders contributed greatly by increasing the number of people I was able to contact and secure interviews with. Jim's ability to locate people was amazing. I'd give him a name and more often than not he'd come up with a phone number.

Thanks also to English teacher, author, and friend Shaunna Howat; my daughter, Faith, for editing help; my son, Micah, for technical assistance; and my nephew, Brian Varick, for help with graphics.

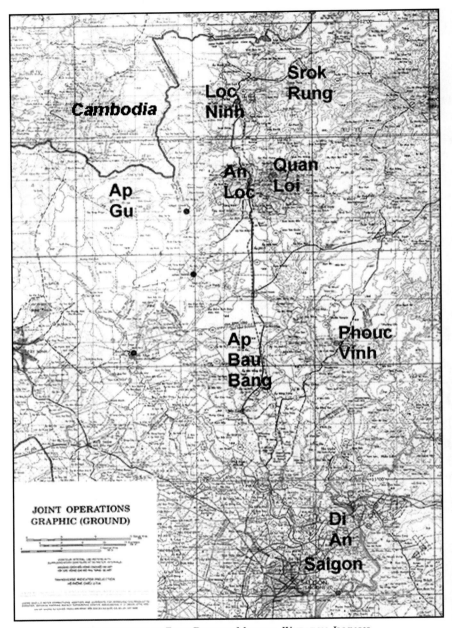

Cambodia

Loc
Ninh

Srok
Rung

An
Loc

Quan
Loi

Ap
Gu

Ap
Bau
Bang

Phouc
Vinh

JOINT OPERATIONS
GRAPHIC (GROUND)

Di
An

Saigon

MAP COURTESY OF FIRST DIVISION MUSEUM, WHEATON, ILLINOIS.

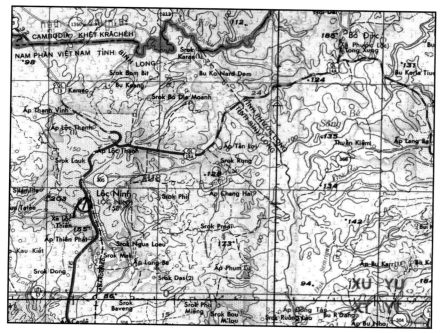

Map of the northern area of the 1st Infantry Division's area of operations along the Cambodian border. Loc Ninh is at center left with Srok Rung up and to the right just above the map's center. (MAP PROVIDED BY THE DEFENSE MAPPING AGENCY TOPOGRAPHIC CENTER, WASHINGTON, D. C.)

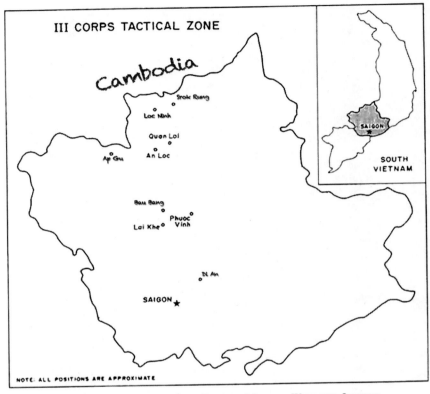

III CORPS TACTICAL ZONE

Cambodia

Srok Rung
○ Loc Ninh
○ Quan Loi
○ Ap Gu ○ An Loc

Bau Bang
○ Phuoc
○ Loi Khe ○ Vinh

○ Di An

SAIGON ★

SOUTH
VIETNAM

SAIGON ★

NOTE: ALL POSITIONS ARE APPROXIMATE

MAP (ADAPTED) FROM THE FIRST DIVISION MUSEUM, WHEATON, ILLINOIS.

Introduction

In 1169 B.C., a horde of Midianite invaders lay encamped on the eastern edge of the lands of ancient Israel. Gideon, commander of the Israelite forces, was preparing to come against them with his army of thirty-two thousand men. This story, recorded in the book of Judges in the Old Testament of the Bible, illustrates an important truth. Directed by God, Gideon announced to his men that anyone who was full of fear and trembling could depart and return to his home. Twenty-two thousand departed and ten thousand remained. The ten thousand were men who had a distinguishing quality in their nature. They were in possession of a character trait that enables men to shrug off fear and function effectively even in the face of grave personal danger. It was this character trait that was in evidence in several men on November 7, 1967, at the battle near the village of Srok Rung, Republic of Vietnam. There, a hundred soldiers of the 1st Infantry Division were caught in an ambush and fought for their lives and for the lives of their comrades. But that day, some of those men also displayed a degree of valor that can only be characterized as "above and beyond" and their deeds in the battle of Srok Rung deserve to be remembered.

In early 1967 the Communist Viet Cong and North Vietnamese were engaged in developing a bold plan to win the war against the Americans and the South Vietnamese. They would change their tactics from unconventional guerrilla fighting to conventional warfare. They would attack ARVN (Army of the Republic of Vietnam) and American bases throughout the country with the goal of overrunning them or at least hemming in the South Vietnamese and U.S. forces while they would take over Saigon, Hue, and other major cities. The plan counted on the South Vietnamese people seeing the Communists as liberators and rising up against the Americans and the South's "puppet" government. If Saigon fell, it was "war over." The plan required utmost secrecy and coordination. The timing would take advantage of the Tet (Vietnamese Lunar New Year holiday) cease-fire in January to catch their enemies with their guards down and at their most vulnerable moment: a large portion of the ARVN forces would be on leave for the holiday and the Americans would be less vigilant during the cease fire.

The enemy's strategic plan included an October attack on a small, remote U.S. Special Forces base close to the Cambodian border. By making a determined, sustained effort against the base, the Americans would be forced to respond. The primary objective was not to seize the base per se, but to foment a major conflict at that location. This would draw American forces away from the northern approaches to Saigon in order to counter the major threat in the border region. The result would afford their forces less fettered access to the city and greater opportunity to secure their foothold in the more populated areas in and around Saigon once the Tet Offensive had begun and before the Americans had a chance to react.

CHAPTER 1

Replacement

I FLEW TO VIETNAM IN JULY 1967. I arrived in the middle of the night aboard a Boeing 707 with a planeload of other military replacements at Bien Hoa Air Force Base fifteen miles northeast of Saigon. The air was warm and humid. Flares lit the sky off in the distance and occasional artillery fire pierced the early morning stillness. We boarded buses and traveled on narrow roads through slum-like neighborhoods. I noticed that the bus windows were covered with wire mesh. I had ridden in plenty of military buses before, but the wire mesh was something new. The purpose quickly dawned on me though—protection against hand grenades. It was a short bus ride to a nearby base where we were directed to a barracks complex and were able to get a couple of hours sleep before the dawning of our first day in country. At morning and afternoon formations, names were called out and unit assignments were announced. On the second day I received my orders for the 1st Infantry Division. At the designated hour a large group of us would be sent by truck convoy to division headquarters at Di An (pronounced "Zee On") several miles away. We were given helmets, flak jackets, and M14s. We threw our duffle bags up and boarded the open deuce-and-a-half trucks and headed to the base camp.

The trip to Di An afforded my first good look at this strange land half a world away from home. The streets outside the base were crowded with American military vehicles and Vietnamese civilians and military personnel riding bicycles, motor bikes, and motor scooter taxis. The civilians wore loose-fitting black or white pajama-like clothing and conical shade hats. The traffic grew sparse as we traveled further and further into the country. The sights were impressively picturesque. I wished that I had a camera. Except for the light brown of the thatch on small country dwellings, lush greenery was present everywhere: bamboo, coconut palms, banana palms, and tropical trees and shrubs of amazing variety. Flooded rice paddies, water buffalo, ox carts— scenes of the orient that I had only experienced in pictures were now combined with smells totally new to my nostrils in a multisensory reality that contrasted sharply with the world I had left behind.

After a few days in the 1st Division replacement station at Di An, I was assigned to a unit at the 1st Brigade base camp at Phuoc Vinh, thirty-five miles to the north. This time I would travel by airplane. Actually, it was more like an albatross with twin engines, called a Caribou. It was a cargo plane designed to fly slowly and to take off and land on short, rough runways. Again, I was instructed to draw helmet, flak jacket, and M14 and to report to the airstrip. I asked what the M14 was for since I was flying. The reply was matter-of-fact: "In case the plane goes down." Oh fine. That was just what I needed to hear. Especially, on top of the fact that I was the only replacement being sent to Phuoc Vinh on that particular day. I guess apprehension was kind of written all over me as I stepped on board, because the crew chief made a special attempt to reassure me that it wasn't all that bad "up there."

My unit was Company A, 1st Battalion, 26th Infantry Regiment (the Blue Spaders.") The 26th Infantry's moniker derived from the unit's distinguishing insignia, a blue arrowhead on a white shield. When I arrived at Alpha Company's headquarters, I reported to the office, was assigned to a barracks, and told to report to the supply room to trade my M14 for an M16 and draw jungle fatigues and other combat gear. Most noteworthy about this experience was the supply sergeant. He was constantly gazing downward and rubbing the back of his neck. The guy was a nervous wreck!

I found the company area mostly deserted. The battalion was out on an operation at the time and besides the supply sergeant, the headquarters clerk, the company executive officer (XO), a few cooks, and a couple of guys getting ready to rotate back to the states, that was it. I was told that before I could join the company in the field I would have to go through a jungle training course and to just hang loose until the next class started in a couple of days.

The Blue Spader battalion compound was located along the perimeter, which consisted of an earthen berm about four or five feet high. Sandbagged bunkers were built into the berm. The area outside the bunker line had been cleared of vegetation for two hundred meters. Multiple rows of concertina wire comprised a barrier that traversed parallel to the berm line. Beyond the wire, a stream, flooded by monsoon season rains, passed through the middle of the open area. Jungle loomed one hundred meters or so past the edge of the water. Off to the left, a couple of thatch roofed "hootches" stood at the edge of the jungle.

That first night I turned in to go to bed in the empty barracks. It was hot and humid and, because my bunk had mosquito netting, I decided to sleep in my underwear. Sometime during the night I awoke to the sounds of explosions going off some distance away. The short time that I had been in country I had gotten used to the fact that our artillery batteries could go into action at any time day or night and it had become a familiar sound. But something about these explosions was different. In a matter of seconds I was wide awake as I realized . . . this was incoming! And the explosions were getting closer! I dressed as fast as I could and put my boots on without socks and without lacing them. It would be the last time I would sleep without clothes and boots on my feet for the next year except for R and R (six day Rest and Recuperation leave). I grabbed my M16 and harness with extra magazines and headed for the closest bunker just a short distance outside the barracks. Already inside the bunker, the supply sergeant stood positioned at the right gun port and he informed me that we had to watch for a possible ground assault. The bunker I jumped into turned out to have a .50 caliber machine gun positioned in the left firing port. I moved up close to the opening to get the best possible view and peered out into the darkness. By now, explosions were going off throughout the company compound to our rear. Phuoc Vinh was undergoing a massive mortar and rocket attack. As I was scanning the narrow arc of territory that comprised the machine gun's firing lane, I saw sparks—red sparks flying into the air above the roofs of those hootches just to the left within my field of fire. Viet Cong mortars! I could hear the "pop" of the rounds as they were being launched from the mortar tubes raining death and destruction on our base—distance, three to four hundred meters—well within range of the .50! I locked a round into the chamber and grabbed the aiming handles to point the machine gun in the direction of those mortars. Tracers would allow me to put the fire right on target, smashing through those hootches and onto the enemy gunners. They were like sitting ducks in a shooting gallery! Just as I was about to press the thumb trigger a violent force slammed me away from the gun!

"Simms! What are you doing? You fire that gun and you give our position away!" I was dumbfounded. This was war! Those mortars needed to be taken out. But my antagonist was a sergeant and I was a private. I had to acquiesce to rank. But how do you win a war with soldiers like this guy, more concerned with his own skin than anything else, regardless of the cost? The wisdom in Gideon's directive to separate out those full of "fear and trembling" accompanies the memory whenever it resurfaces. I've relived this episode in a thousand dreams, but it always turns out the same. Should I have asserted my size and strength over the supply sergeant and sent those enemy mortar crews to their reward? How many lives and limbs and how much materiel could have been saved?

As it turned out, the rocket and mortar attack was not followed with a ground assault, but the next morning revealed some of the consequences. Our company area hadn't sustained any major damage, but the headquarters building and a couple of the barracks had been peppered with shrapnel. No direct hits, and fortunately, with almost the whole battalion out in the field there were no casualties for the Blue Spaders. I never heard the casualty or damage assessment report for the base as a whole, and I was not at liberty to wander around the base, but I did hear that there were a number of casualties and saw helicopters and fixed wing aircraft that were damaged or destroyed on the airfield.

The next few days things were quiet at Phouc Vinh. With a bunch of other new guys, I attended the base's three-day jungle training school. We attended classes which included the people and culture of Vietnam and the nature of the local Viet Cong and their tactics. We zeroed the sights on our M16s and learned how to use the PR-25 field radio. I got firsthand experience on how it would "kick your butt" when its twenty-five pounds is added to the weight of the normal combat pack (I was assigned to carry it on my first training patrol outside the base perimeter). At the conclusion of jungle school we joined the ranks of our respective units—"new guys," with a lot more learning to do.

CHAPTER 2

Always a Blue Spader

IT HAD BEEN SOME THIRTY YEARS SINCE I had come back from Vietnam when I received a letter from a former squad leader inviting me to join my wartime unit's regimental association. "Once a Blue Spader, Always a Blue Spader" was the association's slogan, but I was not ready to revisit that chapter of my life. The fact was that when I came back I wanted to forget a lot of that experience. I didn't mind talking about Vietnam if the subject came up. I had strong opinions about the war, especially in the political realm. I was outraged at John Kerry calling all Vietnam veterans war criminals. I knew the truth. None of the guys in my unit was a war criminal, and I didn't see a violation of the Geneva Convention in my twelve months in country. The Communists were the war criminals. It was the Communists that used assassination, murder, and terrorism against the South Vietnamese citizens in order to "unite" their country. I saw some of their crimes with my own eyes and heard of more from first-hand witnesses. And as for Jane Fonda and others of her ilk giving "aid and comfort to the enemy," whatever happened to the concept of treason? Yet, when it came to my personal experience, painful memories and images had too often sprung up on their own, and that was disturbing enough. Joining the association would certainly worsen the problem. It took a couple of years of contemplating the idea and reading a complimentary copy of the *Blue Spader Newsletter* before I decided to attend a meeting. The fact that it was to be held in Chicago, which was only a six-hour drive from my home in Cincinnati, helped. Also, the bonus that my old friend Charland would be there.

Jim Charland was my first squad leader and the guy who had introduced me to the realities of the jungle. I remember well when he took time to tutor me in the natural wonders of the region—"wait-a-minute" vines with sharp hooks that would grab hold of you as you passed by, millipedes that would raise welts if they walked on your skin, and roots that glowed in the dark. When I expressed some doubt as to the truthfulness of his nature lesson, you might say he wasn't happy. Actually, he kind of exploded in a tirade of indignation because I had questioned his veracity. Well, it wasn't long before I learned that he wasn't putting me on—everything he had told me was true. I looked forward to seeing him again.

Well, that reunion turned out to be quite eventful. Although Jim was the only member from my company at the meeting who was in country the same time that I was, a large contingent of guys from Company C was. I soon learned why so many of them were in attendance.

CHAPTER 3

Blue Spader Reunion
Chicago 2001
Reminiscing

THE CHICAGO REUNION TOOK PLACE THIRTY-FOUR YEARS after the events that had stamped the experiences of those days indelibly in my memory. Now, I was rubbing elbows with survivors of a battle that I had revisited innumerable times in my head. I was a member of Alpha Company, 1st Battalion, 26th Infantry Regiment, 1st Infantry Division. We were the reserve force that had remained back at our night defensive position (NDP) the morning of November 7, 1967, while Charlie and Delta companies, together with the battalion command group went out on patrol. There were heavy concentrations of Viet Cong and North Vietnamese forces in the area, and our battalion's mission was to try to locate and to engage them.

In the early afternoon we got word that radio contact with the battalion had been lost. We were to "saddle up" and be ready to move. Shortly, radio contact was reestablished. The battalion had been caught in an ambush and was pinned down. Part of the message received was "if you don't get here soon, we'll all be dead." We were to move quickly "and be watchful for enemy up in the trees."

In the four months since I arrived in country, my company had experienced its share of rocket and mortar attacks by the VC, but no major ground confrontations with them. In that time we had lost two men KIA (killed in action); one in September when one of our ambush patrols was itself ambushed just outside our NDP and another in October when the company bumped into an enemy base camp deep in the jungle. Now the likelihood of larger scale combat loomed before us. Our thirty-man platoon departed the perimeter with the urgency of our mission and the flow of adrenalin overriding any reluctance based on fear or anxiety. We were moving quickly. I was up near the front, the forward flanker on the left side of the column. At the time I was carrying an M79 grenade launcher. I had recently given up my M16 for the 79. Even though it was a liability in the dense jungle, I liked it.[1] At least it was reliable. I knew that when I pulled the trigger it would fire. My M16 had tended to jam, and I had little confidence in it. The last thing that I wanted was to find myself in a firefight with an inoperable weapon.

After a short period of travel in jungle we broke into rubber. With the increased visibility of the rubber plantation with the trees evenly spaced in rows and the undergrowth kept low, the column spread out and I moved further to the left, increasing the distance between me and the main column to my right.

With all senses tuned to looking for signs of the enemy, and paying special attention to the trees, my scanning eyes were drawn downward and fixed on the incongruity of a long, straight line along the ground in front of me . . . a trip wire . . . booby trap! With no time to alert superiors (normally we would have stopped the column and safely blown the device), I alerted the flanker behind me and kept moving. A short way further and we were getting close. I could hear helicopter gunships firing some distance ahead. Soon I was able to see the choppers as they swept low over the treetops firing rockets and machine guns. Then a shocking scene—several bodies scattered on the ground. Still, lifeless forms lying askew where they had fallen. This was the command group. Among them I recognized the battalion commander's two RTOs (radiotelephone operators). They were lying next to each other. Their clothes were ripped open and they appeared to have been slashed with swords. Then I realized that these were grazing wounds from bullets or shrapnel that had laid open the flesh as from a sharp blade. One of the radios had three bullet holes in the center of it. A section of the fiberglass case of the other radio had been turned to powder by an RPG (rocket propelled grenade) blast! A short distance away, a faceless body lying on its back. It was the colonel! Our battalion commander was dead!

The impact of seeing Col. Arthur D. Stigall with a massive head wound was particularly painful. I had known this man and had looked up to him with a great deal of respect and affection. Just a week or two earlier our battalion had been on perimeter guard duty at the division's northernmost base at Quan Loi. Base camp guard was relatively good duty. We would man the bunkers on the perimeter at night and send out patrols into the surrounding countryside during the day. Patrol duty was rotated among the platoons so some would be given the day off to rest, visit the Enlisted Men's Club (for a 3.2 percent beer), or whatever. Because of increased enemy threat in this area, the colonel had given orders that all of his men within the base were to carry individual weapons and wear their helmets at all times. The usual relaxed rules that governed base camp stays were thereby amended. Nobody was happy about that order. Relief from the constant weight of the helmet was one of the simple pleasures that we looked forward to when we came in from field operations. A friend and I

---

1. The M79 grenade launcher was relatively useless in dense terrain. Although rifle grenades were designed to travel twenty-five meters before they armed themselves and then explode on impact, they could strike trees or brush short of their intended target and expose the person firing them and those around him to shrapnel. Standard operating procedure in the 1st Infantry Division was to unload them in the thick jungle and rely on a .45 semiautomatic handgun for self defense.

decided to ignore that order and left our "steel pots" behind as we headed off to some unremembered location. We were walking on the open ground next to the airstrip when we noticed a jeep on the other side of the runway traveling in the opposite direction. We grew apprehensive when we noticed it circle around and head toward us. Our emotions turned to dread as the jeep got close enough to reveal the insignia on the helmet of the person in the passenger seat—the colonel! We instinctively saluted as the jeep came to a stop.

"Where are your helmets men?" We were speechless. What could we say?

"What company are you men in?"

"Alpha, sir."

No further questions; he calmly told us to jump in and instructed his driver to head for the Alpha Company headquarters tent. Our CO, Capt. James E. Altmeyer, was summoned, and we knew we were in deep trouble. When he emerged, he saluted the colonel and was informed of our noncompliant status, and that was it. As Colonel Stigall's jeep sped off Captain Altmeyer asked us where our helmets were and told us to go get them. That was all there was to it—what a relief! In retrospect, our helmet order violation was small potatoes compared to the gravity of the strategic situation in this region of Vietnam that we were not privy to as low level enlisted men. Yet, to us at the time, it was a huge act of mercy.

Something else about Lieutentant Colonel Stigall distinguished him as a leader. As a battalion commander, he didn't have to be on the ground with the troops. He could have been up in a helicopter out of harm's way monitoring the situation and directing the unit, especially in light of the fact that he had recently broken his ankle and was wearing a cast. No one would have faulted him for not being on the ground, but he was a selfless commander with a devotion to duty and chose to be close to his men, a walking cast fitted to his leg.

Now he was dead—this gentle officer that wore a CIB with two stars.[2] A combat veteran of World War II and the Korean War killed in action in Vietnam. Questions flooded my mind. What could have happened here? How could the command group positioned in the most protected place in the column have been so devastated? How did the normal tactical measures designed to detect ambushes fail? As the situation required immediate action my questions would have to wait. With the enemy having broken contact, the task at hand was to secure the area and evacuate the wounded as soon as possible. I was assigned to the latter task.

Lying a few yards from the battalion commander was a soldier with a bullet wound to his stomach, a single round hole and no exit wound. Pale, and his midsection swollen from internal bleeding, his condition did not look good, but he was conscious and able to talk. With only two of us to carry him we had to remove our combat packs to lighten our load so that we could concentrate on

---

2. CIB: the Combat Infantryman Badge, the much-respected award for having served in a combat occupational specialty in a war zone for at least thirty days.

bearing him to the evacuation point. To say that being in that area without a weapon was an insecure feeling would be an understatement, but we just couldn't carry him and our gear at the same time. Actually, we felt naked. It's amazing how much comfort and security your personal weapon provides when the enemy is near. Without it the contrast was pretty striking. But now personal safety was not an issue. Getting this soldier to the life-saving medevac choppers was our primary concern.

After delivering him to the evacuation area we headed back to our starting point and were directed next to remove Colonel Stigall's body. As we approached the area where the dead were being collected, the magnitude of our losses became apparent. The bodies were laid out in two long rows and we placed the colonel down at the end of one of the rows. It was a demoralizing blow. Some had ponchos covering them. Others lay on their backs with eyes closed as though asleep. These guys were among those that I had observed just a few hours earlier as they headed out on their patrol. I had watched them as they formed up into columns and stepped over the coils of concertina wire that marked the edge of our NDP. These were dutiful warriors; each knew the degree of peril that existed outside the relative sanctuary of the perimeter. Each ventured out to face whatever lay ahead. Now, they were inanimate, still, their lives terminated in this place so far from their families and everything they held dear. The shock was made worse by the appearance of one soldier in particular. His short hair stood straight on end and he had a scream frozen on his face. The thought that accompanied that moment remains coupled with its picture in my memory, "What on earth had he experienced as he met his end?" I did not know the actual extent of our losses until thirty-six years later when I read the official casualty report at the First Division archives in Wheaton, Illinois: eighteen KIA and twenty-two WIA. The killed in action included fifteen Blue Spaders, three artillerymen from the 1st of the 5th Artillery, and the battalion Vietnamese interpreter (For some reason the interpreter was left out of the numbers. The actual count was nineteen KIA and twenty-two WIA).

It was getting dark by the time mop-up at the battle scene neared completion, the last task of which was to dispose of a large pile of damaged and bloodied gear that had belonged to the dead and wounded. Gasoline from chain saws that had been used in an effort to clear a landing zone was poured over the pile, and it was set on fire. At this point higher-ups were engaged in a debate: Should we spend the night in place or try to get back to the relative security of our NDP (night defensive perimeter)? The decision was made in favor of getting back. The march would be perilous. The likelihood of a follow up attack was high, but our vulnerability would be greater by giving the enemy time to regroup and to exploit our situation. Indeed, we were being watched. The rear security element spotted three or four individuals shadowing us. A burst of M16 fire directed at them shattered the quiet and put everyone at the ready wondering if the battle was starting again. Word quickly spread about what had transpired and thumbs moved away from safety switches on M16s and M79s.

We would be moving back in two columns on a straight line to the NDP. It was almost dark as the columns began to move. Within a few minutes it was completely dark, total blackness. Any light from the sky was completely blocked by the jungle canopy above. Our orders were to keep the formation tight, stay within arms length of the man ahead, "Hold on to him if you have to." Given the circumstances, we couldn't afford to have any part of the column get separated.

The march back was made memorable by a masterful use of artillery fire. The artillery base firing in our support was located to the rear of our line of travel. The flight of each volley was audible as the shells cut through the air above the treetops and then impacted, exploding in a deep red fireball visible some distance to our front. Shrapnel ripped through the rubber trees over our heads. I remember thinking that it would be a miracle if we got back with no one being hit. Volley after volley literally blasted clear our rout back. Close in artillery support was perilous but at the same time comforting, given the circumstances that we were in. We made it back without incident, and it was a great relief to step over the concertina wire at the edge of our perimeter. We were heading for our sector of the NDP when an explosion erupted behind us. We turned and readied for action as word was immediately passed up: "Accidental discharge from a grenade launcher. Carry on." We later learned that one man had been wounded by the grenade blast, but not severely. When we got to our position we were greeted by the unfamiliar voices of guys from another unit, 1st Battalion, 16th Infantry, who had been airlifted in to take over the perimeter. We would be given the night off.

The soldiers manning our positions wanted to know what had transpired out there. "NVA [North Vietnamese Army] ambush, lots of dead and wounded, battalion commander dead, Charlie and Delta company commanders dead" (Actually, both company commanders had been wounded and medevaced; I had erroneously been told that they had been killed).

The following is an excerpt from a letter written by Alpha Company radio-telephone operator (RTO) Charlie Macolino to his wife on November 8. It contains a couple of inaccuracies: KIAs (killed in action) were nineteen and, as I had been misinformed, the two company commanders were not killed, but had been wounded and survived.

Hello Honey,

To start with let me say that I am fine. I guess by now you have heard or read about our fight yesterday. There were 18 killed and 25 wounded. Out of the ones killed were the battalion commander, the artillery commander, 2 company commanders, and a first sergeant. Because of all the high ranking people killed we were withdrawn.

We are now near Lai Khe. We will be here until we get re-organized. That should be 3 or 4 weeks.

That was it. We were not in a mood for talking. In fact, I don't think we talked about what had happened that day again. It was now behind us, best to leave it there. The questions about what had occurred on November 7 would remain in my head, unanswered, for thirty-four years. The answers resided with these guys from Charlie Company. The reason that they were at the Chicago reunion in such a large number was that they had forged some very strong bonds as a result of all that they had experienced together in their yearlong tours of duty. In fact, in addition to November 7, some of them had been in the battle of Ap Gu, (March 31–April 1,1967, one of the largest individual battles of the war); the Communist Tet Offensive beginning January 30, 1968; and in the subsequent spring counter offensive. They had maintained contact with each other and had decided to get together again at the Chicago regimental reunion.

In talking to the Charlie Company veterans about November 7, it was as though I was transported back in time. So with their commentaries, and seeking out and interviewing other key people from the battle, combined with the records from the 1st Infantry Division archives in Wheaton, Illinois, outside Chicago, I was able to piece together this story of what has come to be known as the battle of Srok Rung. It is a story that involves a fateful error in judgment, a warning ignored, and a combination of skillful leadership, many individual acts of heroism, and valor above and beyond the call of duty that kept a bad situation from becoming a disaster with a much greater loss of life.

CHAPTER 4

The Siege of Loc Ninh, 1967

THE SPECIAL FORCES CAMP AT LOC NINH[3] lay about ten miles from the Cambodian border some seventy miles or so north of Saigon. The large rolling hills of the region contrasted sharply with the mostly flat terrain which characterized the lower part of the 1st Infantry Division's area of operations. No rice paddies here; the dense jungle and rubber plantations in this part of the country yielded a canopy which, from the air, provided complete obscurity for whatever might be going on at ground level.

A few miles to the north and west, the lower stretches of the Ho Chi Minh trail through Cambodia brought weapons, supplies, and North Vietnamese Army (NVA) infiltrators to the southern part of Vietnam. The Loc Ninh Special Forces base had constituted no real threat to them as they had successfully skirted the tiny base for years previously. Unobservable from the air, they had relative freedom of movement in the area. Only if they headed east or south would they be likely to encounter resistance from the denser concentrations of U.S. and ARVN (Army of the Republic of Vietnam) forces protecting the populated regions.

Now the SF camp was under siege. Official records (including previously classified intelligence documents) identify the attacking enemy units as two regiments of the 9th Viet Cong Division, the 272nd and the 273rd, and two regiments of the NVA 7th Division, the 141st and the 165th. The attack on Loc Ninh began just after midnight on October 29. A heavy mortar barrage was followed up with RPG fire and a ground assault.

The first human wave attack was turned back, but a second assault just before dawn succeeded in breaching the perimeter. With one sector of the base occupied by Viet Cong, additional forces were quickly air lifted to the scene to

---

3. A small detachment of U.S. Special Forces soldiers trained there a Civilian Irregular Defense Group (CIDG), a Vietnamese militia recruited from local men.

counterattack and secure the base. When the fighting was over, ninety-two Viet Cong were found dead inside the base's perimeter (for an eyewitness account of the situation at Loc Ninh see appendix 2 for helicopter pilot Paul Pelland's commentary).

For the next several days rocket and mortar attacks as well as ground assaults would continue against the Special Forces base even as four battalions from the 1st Infantry Division and one battalion from the 25th Division were being committed to the area around Loc Ninh. Several major battles and a number of skirmishes ensued. Our battalion would be committed to the action on November 2.

The plan developed by 1st Infantry Division commander, Maj. Gen. John H. Hay, Jr. was to "box" in the enemy and catch them before they had a chance to escape. Two companies of the 2/28 Infantry were placed to reinforce the Loc Ninh Special Forces base. Four other battalions were placed in a rough square around the base positioned at the most probable enemy withdrawal routes. The 2/12 Infantry (from the 25th Infantry Division) was at the northeast corner, the 1/28 at the southeast corner, the 1/18 at the southwest corner, and the 1/26 at the northwest corner. From bases established at these points, daytime patrols would try to locate and engage the enemy. Nighttime ambushes would attempt to block their escape under the cover of darkness.

On November 1, my company commander, Capt. James Altmeyer, briefed the company with a sense of urgency. On this deployment, Alpha Company would be joined by Charlie and Delta companies to operate as a battalion minus-sized force. (less than a full battalion because Bravo Company was deployed elsewhere and would not be accompanying the battalion on this mission). The likelihood of enemy contact was high. Capt. Leonard Tavernetti, Charlie Company commander, had this to say about the pending mission.

> [G]oing to the Fish Hook area, as the border was called near Loc Ninh, had a definite psychological effect on the men of the company. This would mean regulars, NVA, in strength. Old timers recalled the last time the battalion was in the region and the battle of Ap Gu (March 31–April 1, 1967). Those who had heard of the previous night's activity at Loc Ninh relayed that we were definitely going into battle. Everyone had a serious look and chatter was at a minimum. While it was not really necessary to give any extra orders, most of the squad leaders were double and triple checking weapons and equipment as we waited for the helicopters.

On the morning of November 2 we boarded CH-47 Chinook helicopters and flew to Loc Ninh. We landed near the north end of the airstrip and were instructed to immediately move into the rubber on the east side of the runway. I was struck by the physical beauty of the region. Lush green hills stretched to the horizon. Looking to the south end of the gently sloping airstrip I could see the earthworks of the Special Forces base framed by the edges of the surrounding rubber. Pockmarks on the airstrip from mortar and artillery shells testified to the recent fighting. We moved into the wood line where we were surrounded by severely damaged rubber trees. Limbs shorn off by artillery fire littered the ground. Later, some company members told me that they had seen a number of enemy bodies lying in drainage ditches partially concealed by fallen branches that had been pulled over the top of them.

When Charlie Company arrived at the staging area, they were deposited at the south end of the airstrip, near the Green Beret compound. One squad leader related that when they moved into the rubber at their location they were assaulted by the sickening smell of decomposing flesh. Viet Cong bodies lay strewn around the area, remaining where they had fallen in the fighting of previous days. The company's senior medic, Sp5 Ralph Szydlowski, said that he didn't see any bodies where he was, but "you could sure smell them. It was the smell of burned, decaying flesh. I'd smelled it before and you never forget that." Sp4 Bernie Jaworowski, a rifleman in 2nd Platoon, from his location saw a ditch full of stinking, decomposing bodies. Many of them were wearing the green uniforms of NVA regulars. Immediately they requested and received permission to change location to get away from the stench.

After the three companies (A, C, and D) of the battalion were staged at the Loc Ninh airstrip, there was a short period to wait as the landing zone where we were heading was prepped with artillery fire prior to our helicopter assault. Alpha Company would lead the way. The helicopters would be arriving in groups of five, and each would carry seven fully laden infantrymen to the LZ (landing zone). Our objective was just a few kilometers northwest of Loc Ninh, the edge of a wide rectangular open area surrounded by rubber trees. Our arrival met no resistance, and as soon as we landed we headed straight into the tree line and formed up to conduct a search of the immediate area. Just minutes after getting under way, the point element spotted a couple of VC fleeing some distance ahead of our advancing column. Taking no chances of a possible ambush, jet bombers were called in to strike the area to our front. One bombing run was so close to our position that I could feel the heat of the bursting napalm on my face. Soon we were under way again but found no further sign of the enemy. Our patrol took us within sight of a large village (Ap Thanh Phu) in the middle of the rubber, but for unknown reasons we did not attempt to check it out. This first patrol was kept short. We had a defensive position to construct. We headed back to the landing zone area to begin the work of building our three-man fighting positions.

A long night of digging lay ahead. A couple of feet of topsoil and red clay gave way to a dense compaction of gravel called laterite.[4] The stuff was more like concrete than soil and impervious to shovels. It required a strong blow from a pick or mattock just to loosen a small amount and several blows to make a shovel full. Our company's rule was no sleep until our bunkers were complete with two layers of sandbags for overhead cover. While we were digging in, a

---

4. A clay rich in aluminum and iron oxides formed by decomposition of the ores in warm, moist climates.

Chinook helicopter brought in a 105mm howitzer. Immediately, it was set up inside the edge of our perimeter which extended into the clearing where we had landed earlier in the day. As soon as it was ready, the gun crew began firing into the rubber trees at the opposite corner of the open field. Someone had spotted something. Enemy showing themselves to try to lure us into an ambush? I could only speculate. Again, we weren't informed about the whys and the wherefores of command decisions. My brain was thirsting for information but had to carry on without it. Briefings to inform us of the current situation were rare, and intelligence reports were for officers, not enlisted men.

The digging continued as darkness fell. The process was drawn out because we only had two picks per squad and there was no progress to be made without the picks. As soon as enough ground had been broken up requiring a shovel they were passed to the waiting hands of someone from the adjacent holes. It's ironic how fortunes changed. That very morning as we were preparing our gear for the mission, no one wanted a pick. They were heavier and more cumbersome to carry than a shovel. Now, it was the most valuable commodity in the NDP. Our excavations continued into the night aided by illumination rounds (flares that floated down on little parachutes) fired from the nearest artillery fire support base. It was well past midnight when we completed the second layer of sandbags on our position. Not much sleep that night. With one man at our three-man fighting position having to be awake at all times and 100 percent alert (everyone awake) at 0500 hours, it was an hour or maybe two.

The day dawned without incident. It was the morning of November 3. The battalion minus search-and-destroy patrol went out. No enemy contact, but a base camp was discovered with seventeen newly constructed bunkers. It also came across an oxcart trail in the rubber and alongside it a recently used campfire with empty ration cans.

On November 4, in midmorning, four to five VC with packs were seen fleeing before the point squad of the battalion minus column and were able to escape. In the early afternoon a small bunker complex was discovered containing eleven fighting positions and an eight-by-eight-foot command bunker with commo wire running in all directions. Also found in the camp were bloody clothing, two Chinese made .50 caliber machine gun rounds, cooking equipment, and seven pounds of rice. On the afternoon of the fourth the battalion reconnaissance platoon conducted a search of the village we came across on the first day of the operation. Villagers told the battalion interpreter that forty to fifty VC were in the village the day before we arrived on the second.

On the morning of November 5, the patrolling routine was changed. The VC were obviously avoiding us. Instead of two company—battalion minus search-and-destroy—patrols we would conduct much smaller platoon-sized patrols. We could cover more territory and perhaps entice the enemy to engage. Several patrols (approximately twenty men strong) were sent out to search the surrounding area. I was walking my usual flank security position on the left side of our single column formation. That morning our patrol was conducted completely in the rubber. Midmorning the formation halted. I saw our point man turn and call out to our platoon leader:

"Sir! There's a base camp up here!"

The point man was within sight just a short distance ahead of me and to my right. I surveyed the area but could see nothing to indicate a base camp. He was instructed to proceed. We moved slowly, cautiously, weapons at the ready. Thumbs on safety switches.

As I advanced a few paces further, I began to discern the situation: bunkers! Bunkers to the front of me, bunkers to the left of me, bunkers to the right of me; and I wondered, were there bunkers behind me that I had missed? We were in the middle of an enemy base camp and hadn't realized it. I marveled at their skill in the use of camouflage. Fortunately for us, the camp was empty. The column halted and we did a thorough check of the site. A cooking area revealed small hand-held eating bowls with rice still in them. Whoever was here made a hasty departure some time before our arrival. The question was, where were they now? When the column began moving again it was with a heightened sense of vigilance.

The balance of our patrol yielded no contact and no further evidence of enemy activity. None of the other patrols on the fifth had contact either. That evening listening posts and ambush patrols went out, as was the routine, but all was quiet, "situation negative."

The morning of the sixth, the ambush patrols were called in early. In the battalion's duty log it was recorded that all night elements closed the perimeter by 0555 hours. We were instructed to break camp. The enemy had left the area and we were going after them.

Intelligence reports indicated that at least one of the enemy regiments had managed to slip out of the "box" to the northeast and had them located in the vicinity of the small rubber plantation village of Srok Rung, twelve kilometers northeast of Loc Ninh.

Capt. Leonard Tavernetti, C Company commander, characterized the move to our next destination the following way:

Just like the air assault a few days before, the helicopters swarmed into our pickup zone. Vietnam yielded two contrasts in those days: oppressive heat and pungent smells on the ground, and once in flight, cool breezes and fresh air. There was no enemy contact in the AO [area of operations] at the time, so we had the usual "helpers" from brigade and division watching our assault. Two things we did not anticipate were the height of the elephant grass and the fires which had been started by the white phosphorus rounds from the 105s. This was a signal that the last artillery round had been fired and the [helicopter] gunships were cleared to strafe the LZ [landing zone]. When we went in the helicopter pilots kept the skids of the Hueys about six feet above the ground so most of us fell or jumped from a significant height into the grass.

Sp5 Ralph Szydlowski, Charlie Company, medic:

On November 6 I was in the first wave coming in to the LZ. That was unusual for me because I was the senior medic, but I was in the first group of five choppers. I was with First Sergeant Poolaw and I don't remember who else, but I was the first one out. The skids of the Huey were just six inches above the grass, but it turned out to be elephant grass so I just kept falling. I stumbled when I hit the ground and as I was stumbling Sgt. Poolaw hit my back. He came down right in the middle of my back and I was out. When I came to the entire battalion had completed the landing and they were already digging in.

Cpt. Leonard Tavernetti:

[In the landing] I told the platoon leaders to run their men through the flames into the burned out areas. We assembled in the charred stubble with smoke from the fire concealing our movement from the wood line. After everyone was accounted for, we began patrolling toward our future base camp and then outward in a sweep of our portion of the battalion perimeter. I radioed 1st Sergeant Poolaw to let the fires burn since it would save us from having to clear fields of fire later [and make it more difficult for enemy to sneak in close at night]. Collectively, we all were apprehensive of another Ap Gu with hoards of NVA making a mass assault on our NDP. I wanted to be able to call in air and artillery before they got on top of us. [The battle of Ap Gu, March 31 and April 1, 1967. American casualties: 17 Killed In Action (KIA), 102 Wounded In Action (WIA). Enemy casualties: 609+ KIA, unknown WIA, 5 Prisoners Of War].

This location was at the corner of a large open valley bordered on one side by rubber and on the other by brushy jungle. As the patrols were out checking the surrounding area, the majority of the battalion began constructing the NDP on the high ground at the edge of the rubber. Alpha Company's sector included the quadrant that was partially in the open field facing west and south. The area erupted into a bustle of activity as the work of building bunkers and laying concertina wire proceeded with a sense of urgency. Everyone knew that in all likelihood the enemy was near.

In contrast to the laterite of the previous night defensive position (NDP), the digging here was easy. Constructing our three-man position was completed expeditiously, and it was still light when Lieutenant Colonel Stigall made the final rounds checking the bunker line with the company commanders. On the northern side of the perimeter, which extended into the rubber trees, he had the defenders conduct a live fire exercise. As this sector of the perimeter opened up with M60 machine guns and M16s on full automatic, the interlocking lanes of fire were dramatically illustrated as the red tracers poured from gun ports crisscrossing out into the encroaching darkness. The colonel relayed his approval to the other officers and moved on, satisfied that our defenses were ready for any eventuality.

I had been assigned to listening post (LP) duty that night. Normally, when a unit was in an NDP, each platoon would send out a listening post to the front of its sector of the perimeter. With three companies on this operation there were nine rifle platoons and, therefore, nine listening posts on the night of November

6. When it was almost dark two other men and I packed a radio and headed out across the barbed wire out in front of our position. We selected a spot of open ground in the burned out area and set out our Claymores (hand-detonated anti-personnel mines). A short time after darkness had completely set in, from our vantage point overlooking the valley we observed an air force gunship firing in support of a battle raging two to three miles away. The constant streams of red tracers from the plane's miniguns looked like water spewing from a hose. A solid line of red near the plane separated into individual specks of red when more distant and then spread out into a spray as the multibarreled machine guns showered the area below. The fact that another unit in the area was under a ground assault served to emphasize the need for our own alertness.

Listening post was normally a stressful experience. It was three men and a radio out beyond the barbed wire. No bunker, no overhead cover, no one on our flanks. We were just out there. Stay awake. Watch. Listen. If you detect enemy trying to infiltrate, detonate the Claymores and get out of there. Shout to the men on the bunker line that you're coming in and make for the relative safety of the perimeter. Early warning was key to successfully repelling a ground assault. After midnight only one-third of the men would be awake at any given time. Early warning would give the opportunity to get everyone awake and ready to defend the perimeter.

Pfc. Thomas Dombek, Alpha Company, 1st Platoon, rifleman:

I was on listening post the night of November 6. We were set up in the open area with rubber trees about one hundred yards from our position. VC were at the edge of the tree line all night. We could see the red glow from their cigarettes every time they took a drag. I think they were teasing us, trying to draw fire. We reported our observations, so leadership had to know we were being watched.

Staff Sgt. Albert "Butch" Gearing, Charlie Company, 3rd Platoon, 1st Squad leader (acting platoon sergeant):

On the night of November 6 I smelled marijuana smoke. Thinking that it was our guys I walked the area to check it out, but it wasn't coming from our positions. I went out front of our bunkers and could tell the smoke was drifting in from beyond our bunker line. [As Tom Dombek noted, it had to have been clear to leadership that the enemy was here and in all probability was monitoring our every move. If they wanted to fight they would either attack us in our NDP, which would give us the advantage, or engage us on their terms in an ambush, where they would have the advantage].

If it hadn't been for physical exhaustion, sleep would have been difficult. As it was, when my turn at watch was completed, I woke the next man on duty and drifted off quickly. At some point in my two hours off, however, I was abruptly awakened by an unexpected attack. Sharp, stabbing pain hit me in my legs and groin. I jumped up and ripped down my fatigue pants in an attempt to ward off what turned out to be a type of stinging ants. My two LP mates were doing the same, as they also were under attack. All we could do was swipe them off our legs as best we could in the darkness. Surmising that we had set down on top of a nest of nocturnal predators, we shifted our position a few feet and returned to business as usual. I thought I had seen it all by this time in my tour: black ants, red ants, red and black ants, green ants, brown ants with huge abdomens, biting ants that dropped out of trees as you passed by, and now ants that stung like bees and attacked by night. This place was an entomologist's paradise.

A couple more hours and the sky started to lighten. Before the sun was up above the trees to the east we were ordered to return to the perimeter. As I was coiling up the wire to my Claymore I noticed that one of our mines was aimed in the wrong direction. Instead of aiming out, it was aimed in, right at our position! If we had had an enemy attack during the night we would have blown ourselves away. I questioned its owner, a relatively new guy. He claimed he had placed his Claymore correctly. Either he made an inadvertent error, or enemy had visited us during the night and turned it around.

It was November 7. This day would mark itself in the memories of all the Blue Spaders who were there for the rest of their lives.

November 1967	Operations of Co A, 1-26 Infantry
Thursday 2	C-47 to Loc Ninh SF camp, thence by HU1H to LZ 6 KM NW
Night of 2–3	Dig NDP in laterite
Friday 3	Bn (-) patrol; discover small, recently used enemy camp
Saturday 4	Bn (-) patrol; discover another frequented enemy camp
Sunday 5	Platoon patrols; find large, fortified enemy base camp with signs of hasty departure
Monday 6	Battalion (-) lifted by HU1H to LZ NE of Loc Ninh, dropped into elephant grass
Night of 6–7	Dig NDP; man listening posts (LP)
Tuesday 7	Bn (-) patrol to ESE; Co A remains in NDP

CHAPTER 5

November 7, 1967

THE MORNING OF THE SEVENTH, Lt. Col. Stigall called the battalion staff and company commanders to the normal meeting. He briefed the group on the latest intelligence reports. An NVA regiment was believed to be in the area. The battalion would search for it with Charlie Company's three rifle platoons and two rifle platoons from Delta Company. One rifle platoon from Delta would be on ambush patrol that night and would be given the day off. They were to rest for their night mission and be available to help defend the perimeter should it be attacked. Alpha Company would be in reserve and man the bunker line.

Capt. Leonard Tavernetti, commander, Charlie Company:

> I reminded the Colonel that it was Charlie Company's turn to be the lead company. He laughed and remarked that we were getting a reputation for not wanting to follow anyone. I always rotated the platoons and today it was third platoon's turn to be out front. I gave Lt. Nery [3rd Platoon leader, Manny Nery] the general plan and we selected check points and the route. He was a seasoned platoon leader and I had a great deal of confidence in his leadership. He also had a close relationship with his men. He knew who to put on point, who to put on compass, and who to put on pace. We both knew that with LTC Stigall in our group we had to be as watchful of his oversight as we were of the enemy. It was important to us to look good for the "Old Man."

The battalion would proceed in two columns behind a point squad that would lead the way. As normal, riflemen would move out to both sides of the point element and the main columns to provide flank security. Tavernetti liked this formation. It allowed the unit to have a wider profile as it moved covering more ground and it provided somewhat greater security for the command group which would be positioned between the two companies and in the center of the double column. If the point platoon ran into trouble, men from the trailing columns could easily be directed forward for reinforcement or fill in on the flanks of the lead squad as needed. In open terrain or in rubber the formation would spread out quite far, limiting the amount of damage that could be done by individual weapons carried by the enemy. When men got too close together a single burst from an automatic weapon, rocket-propelled grenade (RPG), or Claymore could take out several. In dense terrain the column would shrink down as men would spontaneously move closer together to maintain visual contact. To more thoroughly check out an area and also to keep from walking into an enemy trap, periodically the column would be halted and small patrols called "cloverleafs" (see next page) would be sent out to recon the area further out to the flanks. The goal was to find out what was in the area in question and to avoid surprises.

Third Platoon was to lead the formation. First Squad of 3rd Platoon would be on point some distance ahead of the double column main body. Lieutenant Nery and his radiotelephone operator (RTO) would be up front with the point element. Second Squad would lead the left column and 3rd Squad would lead the right column. Next in line in the left column was 1st Platoon, and in the right column, 2nd Platoon. Captain Tavernetti and his two RTOs would walk between the two columns. Behind Charlie Company it was Delta Company's 1st Platoon in the left column and 3rd Platoon in the right column (Delta's 2nd Platoon was back at the NDP). Colonel Stigall and the rest of the command group, which included the colonel's two RTOs, the artillery liaison officer and his RTO, the battalion intelligence sergeant, and a Vietnamese interpreter traveled in the center between Charlie and Delta companies.

Sp4 Bob Morris, 3rd Squad of the 3rd Platoon (the lead platoon):

After Lt. Nery received the orders he called the squad leaders over to his bunker and briefed them. He and First Sergeant Poolaw pulled Sgt. Payne [Ron Payne, 3rd Squad leader] aside and said, "Look, let Pope [Sp4 Jim Pope] and Griff [Sp4 Hiawatha Griffin] stay behind and work on the bunkers, they are too short." [Guys whose time remaining in country was drawing to an end.] First Sergeant Poolaw wanted Payne to stay back as well. But Payne wanted this to be his last patrol with his squad and refused to stay back. Lt. Nery pointed out that the platoon was short handed and Payne's leadership was needed. He promised that this would be the last time Payne would go out.

Sgt. Payne returned to our bunkers and gave out squad assignments [for 3rd Squad leading the right column]. Stryker [Sp4 Robert Stryker] would be on point. Willie Omnik, rifleman would be second. Sgt. Payne and his RTO would be next followed by the machine gun crew. Charlie White was the gunner, Johnny Young was assistant gunner, and Larry Banks was the ammo bearer. Doc Faircloth [Sp4 James Faircloth], medic, brought up the rear. Barnett [Sp4 Billie Joe Barnett, Jr.] would be flank security to the right of the squad. I was picked to count the pace as backup to the point squad at the head of the formation. It was that twist of fate that saved my life.

As the battalion was forming up to depart the perimeter, I'm sure that just about everyone had a sense of apprehension as to what they might encounter that day. A member of Alpha Company's mortar platoon remembered it well:

CLOVERLEAF PATROLS
"Find the enemy with the smallest possible force!"

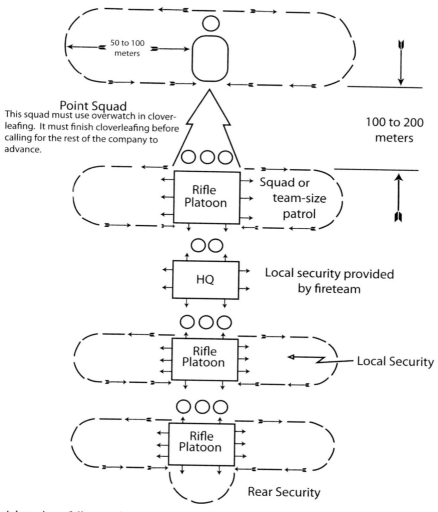

50 to 100 meters

Point Squad
This squad must use overwatch in cloverleafing. It must finish cloverleafing before calling for the rest of the company to advance.

100 to 200 meters

Rifle Platoon

Squad or team-size patrol

HQ

Local security provided by fireteam

Rifle Platoon

Local Security

Rifle Platoon

Rear Security

Adaptation of diagram from *Vietnam Studies: Tactical and Materiel Innovations* by Lt. General John H. Hay, Jr.

Sgt. Gene Mock, Weapons Platoon, fire direction control squad leader:

I had gotten to know the artillery guys pretty well. I remember seeing Dobol 24 [Capt. Michael D. Cochran, B Battery, 1st of the 5th Artillery] and Dobol 24 kilo [Cochran's RTO, John R. Ensell, B Battery 1st of the 5th artillery] as they were getting ready to leave the perimeter that morning and telling them to "come back safe." Both of them looked at me and smiled. Dobol 24 said, "I have to," and then taking out his wallet and showing me a picture of his family. 24 Kilo did the same.

Staff Sgt. Albert "Butch" Gearing, Charlie Company, 3rd Platoon, 1st Squad leader/acting platoon sergeant:

My squad was the lead element. We were out in front of the double column formation which was following some distance behind. Summers [Sp4 Paul Summers] was on point and Baker [Sp4 Edwin Baker, Jr.] was on the compass. Summers always walked point with his pump action, 12 gauge shotgun. Baker packed an M16. I was third in line with my RTO, PFC David Cavazos. The pace man [name unknown] was behind me. Next it was Lt. Nery and his RTO, Sp4 John Bastardi. They were followed by Bob Morris counting pace as a backup and we had two flankers, one to each side.

In the battalion duty log it was recorded that it was 0919 hours when the column moved out. The point element crossed the wire and headed down the slope on the east side of the perimeter and into the scrub brush that comprised the first leg of the patrol. The compass azimuth was, roughly, east southeast. The column was moving slowly, deliberately. The first slope ended in a trickling stream. Summers crossed alone and ascended the slope on the other side to survey the immediate area before giving the hand signal for Baker and the rest of the point squad to proceed. The crest of this hill brought the first leg of the patrol to an end. Here the terrain flattened and transitioned into rubber. The column again halted and cloverleaf patrols were sent out to recon the flanks. Baker took the compass reading for the second leg of the patrol and directed Summers on the new heading. The cloverleafs returned with a negative situation report, and the column was underway again. The compass azimuth was now roughly east. The next objective was a small village,[5] checkpoint two. Point squad members automatically spread the distance between themselves. The double column spread apart and flankers ranged far out to the sides as the relative open of the rubber plantation allowed increased visibility.

Staff Sgt. Butch Gearing:

As we were on our way to checkpoint two, we spotted four VC in black pajamas

---

5. The village was Ap Son Tay. This is confirmed by the battalion Combat After Action Report that notes the coordinates of the village. It has been erroneously identified as Srok Rung in a number of accounts of the battle. Actually Srok Rung, the village from which the November 7 action received its name was the closest village to the battle, approximately 1.2 kilometers east of the battle site.

carrying weapons running out in front of us. Three of us opened up on them with M16s as they fled back towards the village, now in sight, but we couldn't tell if we hit any of them.

Sp4 Bob Morris:

The radios came alive as everyone up the chain of command sought information. "What, who, how many, where?" Instantly, it seemed, the battalion command group was at the front. LTC Stigall, hobbling on that broken foot, was in full command and ready for action. The original plan had called for us to check out the village. Now, it was imperative. The plan was quickly decided upon and we were on the move again, weapons at the ready. The village was sealed and our platoon went in. For as remote as this area was this village was relatively large. There was one narrow main cart path with single family dwellings on either side. When we first came up to it most of the residents were hiding. Shortly, they began gathering out in front of their hootches. It was quiet, very quiet. Not a peep from anyone. Just stares. Fear in the eyes stares. . . . We searched each and every dwelling. Each hootch had a hole in the floor leading to a survival bunker. We really didn't find much of anything except for a packet of white powdery stuff that I found in one of the bunkers. My guess is that it was drugs, but don't know for sure. I passed it on to our senior aid man, Ralph Szydlowski. I thought that it was odd. Why would there be this much hard drugs, if that is what this was, in this village? But then I remembered what we had heard about the NVA using drugs to hype themselves up prior to making a ground assault. As we were going through the village, at some point the Colonel, who was overseeing the search, admonished us to be at the ready with our fingers on the triggers.

Staff Sgt. Butch Gearing:

We didn't find much, but in one of the hootches we found a young man all covered up with a big heavy blanket, and it was hotter than hell. We wanted to check him out to see if he had any bullet wounds, but "mamasan" [adult female] said he was sick and wouldn't let us touch him. We finally got the battalion interpreter in there and he questioned them, but she still would not allow his blanket to be pulled down and nobody forced the issue. I was not a happy camper about it. Chances are high that he was VC and had information and nothing came of it.

The best guess is that he was one of the four seen running toward the village just a short time earlier. It was pretty much unprecedented to find a young man of military age in a remote village. Young men were either in the South Vietnamese army or they were Viet Cong. This guy had probably been wounded and couldn't keep up with the other three who had either fled through the village or scrambled into a hidden tunnel in the area.

Sp4 Bob Morris:

After the point squad had made it through the village we were directed over to the east side to check out a couple of rubber processing structures. A large abandoned storage like building stood by itself. I made my way to the front door expecting to get shot at any moment. I leaped inside the door frame and was greeted with . . . more silence. It obviously had not been used in some time and jungle undergrowth had begun to take over the place. Scattered about the area were many broken ceramic bowls used to collect the rubber sap from the trees. Not a single bowl was intact. It was as if someone had deliberately torn the place apart. Next, we made our way to the rubber processing area. Actually, this was nothing more than an open sided collection of poles holding up a tin roof.

The broken, rubber collection bowls provided more evidence of NVA presence in the area. The French plantation owners seemed to have had some kind of an "understanding" with local Viet Cong units. I surmised that there probably was a peaceful coexistence agreement. The VC would allow the plantations to continue to operate in return for some unknown compensation. Possibly, it allowed them to place their agents, posing as rubber workers, into close proximity to the American bases and thereby get day-to-day information on our activities. For example, the 1st Division's forward base at Quan Loi, twelve miles to the south, was mortared and rocketed often, yet it was amazing how the enemy gunners were able to avoid hitting the plantation owners' homes and buildings. Communists, however, fresh off the Ho Chi Minh trail opposite Srok Rung may not have been aware of or cared about local protocol. The French capitalists were probably on an equal level with the American "invaders" to them.

At this point an interesting side story was developing that involved a Delta Company rifleman. It occurred during one of the times when the column had been halted prior to Charlie Company moving into the village or possibly when Charlie Company was conducting the search of the village. Normally, when a column stops, soldiers tend to sit down and rest. They are carrying heavy combat packs, and most are trying to function with a significant sleep deficit. The average amount of sleep when out in the field was three or four hours per night. It was commonplace in such situations to sit down on the ground, lean up against a tree and doze off. When the word is given to move out you open your eyes, return to wakefulness, stand up and move on. Such was the case for one of Delta Company's rearmost flankers, Sp4 Bill Anderson. He fell asleep and never heard the word to move. When he woke up, he was by himself. The battalion had completed the search of the village and had moved on. When his dilemma dawned on him and as he was looking around and contemplating a plan of action, he spotted three VC walking toward the village just thirty-five to fifty yards away. Fortunately they had not seen him. He decided that the best course of action was to retrace his steps and return to the NDP, which he did without incident. The situation landed Anderson in a bit of hot water and got his squad leader also in trouble for failing to keep track of his men.

CHAPTER 6

Closing In

THE BATTALION MOVED OUT FROM THE VILLAGE around 1230 hours and headed to checkpoint three. The direction of travel continued east. This leg of the patrol would take them along the southern edge of the rubber plantation and a short distance into the jungle beyond the plantation's eastern border. The pace was slow and cautious. The instincts of many told them that the enemy was near. Lieutenant Colonel Stigall had the point squad move out further to the front, two hundred meters ahead of the main column. Staff Sergeant Gearing had his point man thirty to forty meters out front of the rest of his point squad and flankers forty meters or more out to the sides.

Capt. Leonard Tavernetti, company commander, Charlie Company:

Moving in the rubber was a mixed blessing. It was always cooler there and it was easier walking. The natural firing lanes that the rows of rubber trees afforded our enemy was our chief concern. We had a point squad well out in front of our main formation for security against an ambush. Our main formation consisted of one platoon in the lead split into two columns followed by our two other platoons, one on the right and one on the left. Each of these platoons had a flank squad outboard for greater security. The company was in an inverted "V" formation with Delta Company behind us and the battalion command group between the two companies.

The probability of running into an ambush was high. Everyone knew it, but they were ready. The tactical formation of the battalion was designed to detect and react to the threat. Artillery could be brought to bear within minutes of enemy contact. An artillery forward observer was positioned with the lead rifle company, and a liaison officer was with the Battalion Command Group. Charlie and Delta companies' mortar platoons were standing by their tubes back at the NDP ready to provide close-in indirect fire.

The two companies were moving east along the southern edge of the rubber plantation. The right column's flankers were walking between the last row of rubber trees and the jungle to their right that delineated the terrain change. A couple hundred meters short of check point three, when the formation was eight to ten rows of trees from the southeastern corner of the rubber plot, the point group observed three Viet Cong running ahead of the column and into the jungle straight to their front. This information was radioed up the chain of command, and the column halted. Staff Sgt. Butch Gearing, the senior noncommissioned officer in the point squad, suspected an ambush and requested a change of direction. Maps were being checked and location confirmed up and down the command structure probably all the way to division level (cloverleaf patrols should have probed the areas to the front and to the flanks, but for unknown reasons they were not sent out). Alpha Company's CO, Capt. Gene Altmeyer, monitoring the radio traffic from back at the NDP could see that the enemy was trying to draw the battalion into a trap. He relayed his suspicions to Colonel Stigall. The lead element of the column moved forward to within three or four rows of trees from the end of the rubber. They could clearly see the area where the fleeing VC had disappeared. Here the terrain transitioned into low to medium scrub. All was quiet, situation report negative. Except that is, for the pounding of a hundred soldiers' hearts as adrenaline was being pumped into the Blue Spader's veins. Colonel Stigall agreed with Sergeant Gearing's request to change direction. Instead of proceeding on to checkpoint three the battalion would turn here, ninety degrees to the left. The compass azimuth was now approximately north. The change in the route of travel would take a few minutes to coordinate with the Tactical Operations Center. Everyone sat down and rested but maintained vigilance. Shortly, the point group was told to move out.

The forward portion of the patrol was now moving parallel to the eastern edge of the rubber with the right column three or four rows from the jungle. Approximately fifty meters from the point of the turn along the new leg of the patrol, Summers, the point man, spotted a sniper in a tree. Neither he nor the sniper fired. Summers shouted back to Sergeant Gearing for instructions and immediately received the command to shoot! The shot from Summer's 12-gauge shotgun rang out, and the VC dropped to the ground dead. Suddenly, another VC dropped out of a nearby tree and took off running. Baker, number two in line, fired a single shot hitting the fleeing man in the arm. The wounded enemy continued to run off to the column's front and vanished from sight before Baker could get off another shot.

At that point Sergeant Gearing realized that they were in deep trouble and radioed back to keep the column from advancing any further. Third Platoon leader Manny Nery, located at the rear of the point squad, hearing the shots ran forward with his RTO, John Bastardi, and Sp4 Bob Morris. The situation had to be evaluated and decisions made. Further to the rear the main formation was making the ninety degree turn to the left to follow their point squad. When the shots were fired up front the men in the main column spontaneously began moving rapidly forward. Captain Tavernetti with his two RTOs ran to the front so he could better assess the situation.

Meanwhile, back toward the rear in Delta Company's sector a problem was developing. Flankers on the right side of the column were reporting green uniformed men moving quickly toward the column. The problem was that a couple of times on previous operations cloverleaf patrols from the lead company had come back into the column in the trailing company's area, surprising their flankers. They had to be extra discerning, therefore, not to fire on any of their own battalion's men, avoiding friendly fire casualties. Also, the Delta Company[6] men had never seen uniform-clad NVA before, but only black-pajama-wearing Viet Cong. The question arose, could these be South Vietnamese Army soldiers who happened to be in the area? They were being extra cautious. They held fire. But this time those approaching soldiers were enemy, wearing the uniform of North Vietnamese Army regulars!

---

6. Delta came over from the states as a unit in August and was attached to the battalion as a unit. Although it was infused with a number of NCOs that had previous combat experience, none of the flankers that day had experience with North Vietnamese regulars.

CHAPTER 7

The Kill Zone

Sgt. Harold Gilbert, Charlie Company:

> I was in the second squad in the right column on November 7. We had just made the 90 degree turn when the first shot rang out. When we realized what had happened we just started running forward toward the firing to see if we could help out. [As the main body of the column was closing the distance to the point, the order was given to stop and hold their positions, probably as a result of Staff Sergeant Gearing's warning]. We sat down and waited. I was sitting on my steel pot for what seemed to be just a few minutes when it all broke loose on us.

The ambushers had held fire as the point squad passed through their men positioned in the trees, and the main column was drawn into their formation kill zone. Then they opened up. For the soldiers of the 1/26 it was their worst possible nightmare. Enemy fire came at them from three different directions. Big Claymores exploded. Rocket propelled grenades, machine gun, and AK 47 fire rained down on the Blue Spaders. The enemy fire was concentrated on the lead platoon of Charlie Company's right column, the battalion command group in the center which was at that time making the ninety degree turn to the left, and along Delta Company's right flank. A heavy volume of fire was pouring out of the jungle at the edge of the rubber along both legs of the battalion's position and out of the rubber trees across Charlie Company's front.

At the point squad's location, a critical decision was being made. They were searching for the wounded VC when the ambush exploded to their rear. Immediately they began receiving small arms fire from the edge of the jungle on their right flank. Realizing the peril of their position in the open rubber, Sergeant Gearing had the squad get on line and charge from their position in the rubber across a drainage ditch and into the jungle with weapons blazing.

Staff Sgt. Butch Gearing:

> We busted right through them and penetrated about 30 or 40 yards into the jun-

gle. You couldn't see three feet in front of you. We formed a tight perimeter and after some initial shooting the VC near us stopped firing so we stopped to conserve ammo.

Sp4 Bob Morris:

We were clinging to mother earth for all she was worth. Bullets were flying overhead clipping branches and impacting the trees around us. Sgt. Gearing urged us to stay down and stay quiet. Next to me Lt. Nery was holding the handset of the radio. We were told to hold our position pending further orders. Over the radio I could hear cries for help, desperate pleas over a background of explosions and bursts of automatic weapons fire. Radio traffic was chaotic. Protocol went out the window as many voices were trying to get their needs met. The sounds of the battle were deafening at times. Mixed with the sounds of explosions, the whooshing of RPGs could be heard over the back and forth exchanges of their AK47s and our M16s and M60 machine guns.

In the opening volley of enemy fire the battalion command group (seven men) was blown away, all dead or dying. Of the eight members of the lead squad of the right column five were killed and two wounded. Early on in the battle all three flankers on the right side of Delta Company were killed. Enemy gunners were targeting the leaders and the men with radios. The radio antennas marked them as the instruments which brought the devastation from the air. To avoid American artillery and helicopter gunships they had to eliminate the radios or be so close to the GIs as to render their radio directed weapons useless. Delta Company CO Ray Dobbins was also hit early in the battle, pierced through the neck with shrapnel from an RPG. Fortunately, the metal didn't hit anything vital and he was still able to function.

With the loss of the battalion command group and their RTOs, Alpha Company commander, Capt. Gene Altmeyer, and other higher ups from battalion and brigade level that had been monitoring the patrol's progress on the battalion radio frequency were cut off. With the battalion radios gone, Altmeyer and others had to switch to either Charlie or Delta Company's radio frequency to reestablish contact. It was at this point that Alpha Company, in reserve at the NDP, was instructed to saddle up and get ready to move out.

Capt. Leonard Tavernetti, Charlie Company:

When Lt. Nery radioed back that they had spotted a man up in the trees and then another running, I started moving up through third platoon to his position and almost got to Lt. Nery when the ambush erupted behind me and to the right flank of the formation. I told Lt. Nery to hold his position and I ran a semi-circular route back through the left side of the column to where I had left the company headquarters. The distance was about 50 meters. Enemy fire was continuing to come out of the jungle on the right [east] side of Charlie Company and the right [south] side of Delta Company's position.

When the VC and North Vietnamese opened their ambush, the battalion was in the process of turning ninety degrees to the left. Charlie Company had executed the turn and was traveling north. The battalion command group was at the juncture of the turn, and Delta Company was still traveling east. The battalion was in the southeast corner of the rubber plantation so there was jungle to the right flank of both companies. It was from concealed positions in the jungle that the enemy was firing. At Charlie Company's front, numerous enemy were up in trees effecting a U-shaped posture. It was the VC/NVA plan to let the point squad pass through their position before opening up on the main body of the battalion. That is why those that were in the trees held their fire even when one of their comrades was discovered and shot by the point squad. They continued to hold their fire until the ambush was blown a short time later.

Sp4 Charlie White, C Company:

> I was the machine gunner that was bringing up the rear of the squad that was leading the right column. I was four or five guys back from Stryker. We were walking 3 or 4 rubber trees from the edge of the jungle scrub to our right. Shortly after the battle opened Sergeant Payne yelled to bring the gun forward. When I got to Payne he was down laying out flat and our medic, Faircloth, was kneeling over him. I could tell he was in a lot of pain. He told me to move my gun squad out toward the wood line and set up the machine gun there. We took a position behind a rubber tree in the last row ten to fifteen feet from the jungle. Enemy fire was coming from the wood line up and down from our location. Just as I got set up I got hit in the face. A piece of shrapnel shattered my right jaw bone and fractured my eye socket knocking me out of commission. My assistant gunner, John Young, hollered for a medic and he got the gun working. There were bullets impacting all around us.

It was a long time before a medic got to White. "Doc" Faircloth never made it. While he was working on Payne, Faircloth was hit and knocked out of action. During the battle, Young and his ammo bearer, Larry Banks, were also hit. Young kept the gun firing, raking the enemy positions along the edge of the jungle until the barrel "burned up," bending from the excessive heat generated by the constant firing. With the gun out of commission, a wounded Young crawled up to check on Billie Joe Barnett, who was down about ten feet away. Before he could return, Young was struck a second time and killed. Banks lay mortally wounded. With the gun silent and no one around him firing, White feared that their position could be overrun and reached down to ready his .45 but found the holster empty. While he was feeling around for the missing handgun, White was hit again. The enemy bullet struck him in the right hip and as he described it, "threw me four feet into the air." Now everyone around him was either dead or dying.

Pfc. Ken Gross, Charlie Company:

> I was an RTO walking in the right flank near the front. Within thirty seconds of the start of the battle just about everyone forward of me was dead or wounded. White tracers were coming out of the jungle to our right and out of the surrounding trees. I was returning fire at the source of the tracers when I saw our medic [Faircloth] run out past me. He went to work kneeling over one of our wounded

[probably Sergeant Payne]. I did my best to provide covering fire for him, but I saw him flinch a couple of times knowing that he was getting shot, but he never stopped working on the guy. He was phenomenal.

Sgt. Greer Cappello, Charlie Company, squad leader:

My squad was in the right column [the 2nd Squad in the right file]. We were positioned just to the rear of Captain Tavernetti and the rest of the company command group which was walking between the two columns to my left. When the battle opened up it was the most intense firing I'd ever experienced. Mixed in with the intense automatic weapons fire and explosions were the screams of the wounded. It was chaos . . . the most frightening experience that I'd ever had. I was praying . . . promising God everything if he'd save me. If you were any kind of Christian you were praying! Bullets were impacting all around me, zinging through the air, ripping through the brush, and hitting the rubber trees. I was carrying an M14 and I was returning fire on full automatic. Early on in the firefight I spotted one up in a rubber tree about 20 yards away and I kept on firing at him until he stopped moving. He's the only one that I actually saw, but I kept firing at points of enemy shooting, mainly from the jungle to my right front until I ran out of ammo. I'd gone through 20 magazines. Then I started looking for a weapon. I crawled over to a machine gun [Charlie White's gun] that was near me with the crew all dead, but the gun was all shot up. I picked up an M16 that had belonged to one of the gun crew and took the magazines from his ammo pouches and resumed firing.

Sgt. G. B. Gastor, Charlie Company:

I was the lead flanker on the right side of the column. We were a good distance out from the main column, several tree rows, maybe fifty to seventy-five yards. Being that far out from the point of rotation when the formation made the left hand turn, we fell behind and were in the process of trying to catch up when the ambush went off. Before we made the turn I was even with Stryker who was leading Charlie Company's right column. So when the shooting started I was approximately even with the middle of the company's formation. The VC didn't even realize that we were out on that flank. All their fire was directed at the main column. As far as I could tell no rounds were directed at us at all during the initial phase of the firefight. We had been walking along the last row of rubber trees at the edge of the jungle. There was a rise in the terrain as the open ground beyond the last row of rubber transitioned into the thick stuff to our right. The enemy shooting was going over our heads. There was an enormous volume of fire coming out of the jungle from where we were and on up to our front. It was obvious that we were up against a large force. I backed out of the area and joined up with the two other flankers that were behind me. We were moving in closer to the main column when they spotted us and started shooting in our direction. We got down behind a big log that happened to be there. We couldn't tell where the shooting was coming from, but it was close. Then I raised my head one time and I saw this VC swing out from one of the nearby rubber trees and fire a burst from his AK at us. He had a leather strap wrapped around his waist and it was tied back up into the tree. Next time he swung out I got up on my knees and unloaded my shotgun at him. He went limp and was hanging from that strap. Just as I was finishing reloading my shotgun another one dropped out of a tree just eight or ten yards away and started running. I fired and he went down. There was a machine gunner near our position at that point, and I had him come over to the log, and he unloaded with his gun all over the area.

Capt. Leonard Tavernetti:

I moved to the right flank of our formation and crouched down next to Lt. Carnes [2nd Platoon leader, Lt. Byron Carnes]. He stated that 40mm rounds from our grenade launchers were bouncing off the rubber trees and back into our position. Neither of us had experienced incoming RPG rockets before, which is actually what they were. I told him to build up a base of fire by having his troops fire at gun flashes and suspected sniper positions in the trees. I wanted to make sure that our perimeter was intact and told him to check the connection with Delta Company. He moved to his right and I went forward toward the third platoon to see if there was a gap to our front. As I dashed between two trees a bullet hit the top of my right foot and somersaulted me to the ground near one of the machine gunners. I told him to keep firing at suspected enemy locations and reached behind me for the handset of a radio. Both my RTOs always stayed close behind, and when I looked around there was no one there. I knew only one thing could keep them from being there. They had both been hit.

I thought the company was in good defensive position, but I knew we needed to get the artillery brought in if we were going to win this battle [by this time the battalion's artillery forward observer and liaison officer were dead]. I began moving toward the company command post in search of a radio. It took me about ten minutes to low crawl over there with rockets exploding nearby and bullets breaking the sound barrier overhead. I found one of the other radio operators; I think he was from the second platoon. I switched the platoon radio to the battalion frequency but heard no one. Radio communications in rubber trees was always a problem, but we were close enough that I should have been able to hear someone. After a few minutes I remembered that we had switched to the battalion alternate frequency that morning. I made the necessary changes and got hold of our artillery. As was SOP [Standard Operating Procedure] in the 1st Infantry Division, we had walking fires alongside the column as we traveled. I asked to have the artillery walked in toward the battalion at 50 meter intervals. A single round at a time started falling closer to our right flank. I kept walking it in until I could hear the trees cracking above us, and the men around me agreed that it was too close. I made a slight adjustment and had them fire for effect several times. The sound was deafening, and everything from branches to leaves to metal was flying all around us. ["Adjusting fire" is made using only the center, or base gun in a battery of guns. "Fire for Effect" is the firing of the entire battery that has adjusted its aim in parallel along with the changes made by the base piece, expanding the size of the impact area].

I was still worried about our perimeter and moved back toward the third platoon and first platoon boundary. I ran from tree to tree crouching down between dashes. When I got near the flank and was lying on the ground, an RPG hit along side of me. The explosion picked me up and threw me against a rubber tree. At that time I pretty much thought the wounds were fatal, but knew that I had to continue doing what I was trained to do. I started crawling back to the company command post when another RPG exploded right alongside my legs and slowed me down further. I kept crawling toward the relative safety of the makeshift CP when the blast of a third rocket hit me just as I arrived. When I got to the radio at the command post I got hold of Ray [Capt. Ray Dobbins, Delta Company commander] and asked his condition. He said he was hit in the neck but still mobile. I told him I could no longer move and for him to take charge of the battalion. He agreed and I did not talk to him again. I asked for Top [1st Sgt. Pascal Poolaw] and was told that he was dead.

Pfc. Dennis Collins, Charlie Company, medic:

On November 7, I was walking near the rear of Charlie Company's left column. When the shooting started we all hit the ground. Nobody in my area had been hit, but after a period of time our platoon leader came back and said, "Doc! We need you up front. Follow me." We ran from tree-to-tree. Bullets were impacting the trees around us as we moved. The first casualty I came upon was Captain Tavernetti. He had multiple wounds with a major injury to his groin, but he was on the radio calling in artillery. I started an I.V. on him and he begged me not to give him any morphine because he didn't want it to interfere with his ability to control the artillery. I did everything I could for him and then moved on. Later, I did give him morphine just before he was carried out to the evacuation point. [Dennis was drafted as a Conscientious Objector. Because of his religious faith he refused to carry a weapon, yet he served honorably and was highly decorated for valor. During our interview he credited the prayers of his mother and two brothers for his survival. He noted that they were praying for him every day.]

As the battle raged on within the U of the enemy's ambush formation the point squad remained hunkered down beyond the fray to the north. After the surviving leadership started to bring the artillery to bear they wanted to utilize the helicopter gunships for close in support.

Sp4 Bob Morris:

Orders came over the radio: "Put out smoke and plenty of it. The gunships need to know where you guys are." I tossed my smoke grenades to our front and continued marking our position as the other guys in the squad passed their smokies to me. The idea was to give us plenty of room when the gunships began making their runs. With their rockets and machine guns blasting, we wanted support, not death by friendly fire.

Staff Sgt. Butch Gearing:

The first run the gunships made was too close. We could see the bullets from the miniguns impacting in the trees above us. It scared the hell out of me. We had switched radio frequencies so I was able to talk to the gunship pilots. We had smoke out so I wanted to make sure they could see it and to clarify with them exactly where we were located. The one I talked to identified [the color of] our smoke and said, "Ok, I see where you are at," and he added "We can see some of them in the trees. They are right by you."

Sp4 Bob Morris:

At this point, we were feeling frustrated. We had done our part, followed orders but hadn't done much. Lt. Nery was beside himself. Finally, he got the okay to bring 1st squad back to the loosely formed perimeter of what was left of the third platoon.

The squad made its way back to the drainage ditch, looked both ways and dashed across. Then we moved slowly, tree by tree towards the sounds of the shooting which was sporadic now. Smoke was drifting, hanging in the air- the smell of gun powder and cordite [a type of smokeless explosive] with the acrid smell from the smoke grenades combined in a sickening mix. Trees bleeding sap indicated that we were getting close. Lt. Nery shouted that 1st squad was coming in. He received the reply "Over to your right. Stay low. Don't shoot."

Staff Sgt. Butch Gearing:

After a while the shooting died down and we could tell that we were no longer receiving fire directed at us. Then, after the helicopter gunships completed their runs and the artillery started pouring in, we knew that we had our opportunity to rejoin the company. We got up and moved back into the rubber. We circled around and we came in right behind our own platoon. We moved in to plug the holes along the line where our dead and wounded were. The shooting was still going on, but it was sporadic. There were enemy out in the rubber to our front. You could see them moving occasionally. They were our targets. Most of the guys in our platoon were out of hand grenades and were low on ammunition, and we were having to conserve on ammo. When you get down to your last magazine you don't want to waste a single shot.

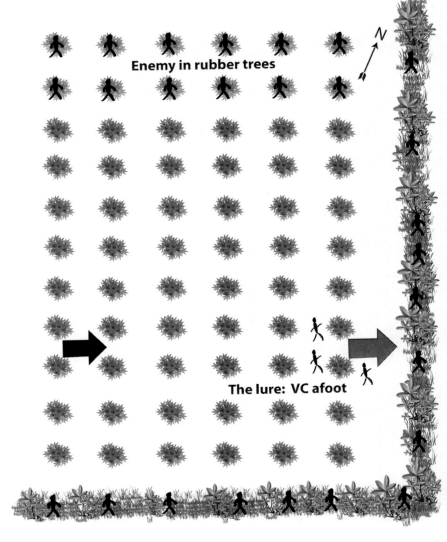

Enemy in rubber trees

The lure: VC afoot

U-Shaped Ambush
3d Battalion, 272d Regiment, 9th "VC" Division

Charlie Company's point squad, 100 to 200 meters out front of the battalion formation, spots three enemy running some distance ahead of their location and disappear into the jungle to their front.

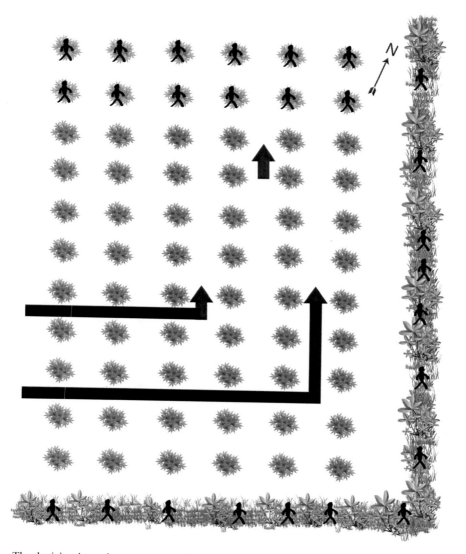

The decision is made not to pursue, but to turn 90 degrees to the left. The enemy, camouflaged and undetected up in the trees to their front, allows the point squad to pass through their position, drawing the main body of the battalion into the kill zone.

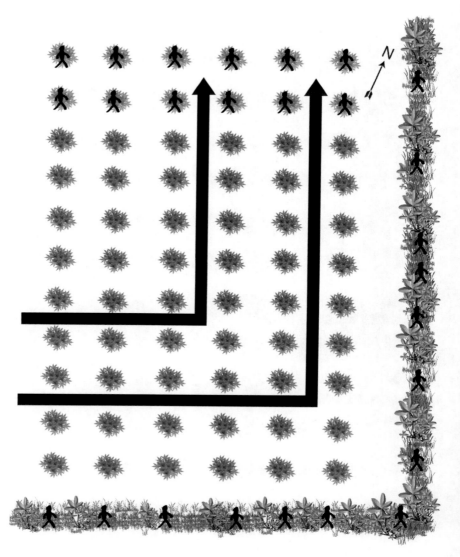

The front of Charlie Company's point squad spots one enemy in a tree and shoots him. Another VC drops out of a nearby tree and runs with the point squad in pursuit. Within seconds the ambushers open up on the main body of the column. The area erupts in a deafening roar as automatic weapons fire and rocket propelled grenades pour in on the Blue Spaders from the surrounding jungle and rubber trees. The battalion command group located between the two columns at the 90 degree turn draws the most intense fire. All seven members are killed within the first couple of minutes.

Lt. Col. Arthur D. Stigall, the Blue Spader battalion commander, was a combat veteran of three wars who extended his tour in Vietnam for an opportunity to command. Officers who served under him described him as a good leader and a very sensitive man who cared deeply about his men. Chaplain John Talley noted that he felt more comfortable with him than any other field grade officer under whom he had served. Charlie Company CO, Len Tavernetti, regarded Stigall as an excellent battalion commander. Delta Company CO, Ray Dobbins, stated that he was the best commander that he ever had.

First Sergeant Pascal Poolaw, combat veteran of three wars (with Purple Hearts from all three), was one of the most decorated Native Americans in U.S. Army history.

One of the few pictures of Bob Stryker that the author was able to find. Bob is on the left. The soldier on the right is Tim Stime (not at battle on November 7). The picture was taken with the soldiers leaning on their combat packs waiting for the word to move to the airstrip for a helicopter assault.

Stryker marking the point with colored smoke. (PHOTO COURTESY OF BUTCH GEARING.)

Company C soldiers on the perimeter at Quan Loi. In the foreground, Capt. Len Tavernetti faces First Sergeant Poolaw (with his back to the cameraman).

Sp4 Bob Morris on the right. Soldier on the left is Jim Myers. He was a new guy that joined Bob's squad early in November. The picture was taken at the battalion compound among the rubber trees at the 1st Infantry Division's base camp at Quan Loi.

Sgt. Butch Gearing with one of the AK47s recovered on November 7.

Staff Sgt. Ray "Tex" Calvert negotiated his way to the front of C Company's right flank during the heat of the battle and came back miraculously unscathed.

Charles E. White, machine gunner on November 7, was wounded twice. He was one of three members of the lead squad at the head of C Company's right flank that survived the battle.

Capt. John Talley conducting a religious service in the field.

Example of what a rubber plantation looks like. This one consists of immature trees.

Sp4 Bernie Jaworowski on patrol outside the battalion's base camp at Quan Loi.

Delta Company commander Capt. Ray Dobbins receiving the Distinguished Service Cross from MACV commander Gen. William C. Westmoreland.

Sgt. Ron Payne, his tour of duty almost at its end, volunteered to lead his squad for one last time. Payne chose to be with his men leading C Company's right column. Plastic bags served as radio handset rain covers.

This is one of the battalion commander's radios from November 7. It was carried back to the NDP and flown to a 1st Division base where this pictured was taken. It is probable that three separate snipers had zeroed in on the radio carried on the radio telephone operator's back. The other RTO's radio was destroyed by an RPG blast.

The Special Forces base and airstrip at Loc Ninh. (PHOTOGRAPH FROM *VIETNAM STUDIES: TACTICAL AND MATERIEL INNOVATIONS*, BY LT. GEN. JOHN H. HAY, JR.)

CHAPTER 8

Green Tracers Coming Down
And Red Tracers Going Up

IT WAS CUSTOMARY FOR THE CHAPLAIN to accompany the battalion when it operated as a unit, and November 7 was no exception. John Talley, the Blue Spader chaplain, would normally travel with the battalion command group.

Capt. John Talley, chaplain:

> I would have been with LTC Stigall, but on the morning of the 7th several of the guys from Charlie Company had asked me to go with them. Everybody was aware that this could be deep stuff. I was near the company command group [Captain Tavernetti and his two RTOs, the artillery forward observer and his RTO, and 1st Sgt. Poolaw] between the two columns. When the ambush opened up there were tracers flying everywhere. I could see green tracers streaking down from several of the trees across my front and red tracers streaming up from our guys as they fired back. After the heavy volume of fire of the initial phase of the firefight died down, two aid stations were set up to treat the wounded and I was helping out at the forward station. There was still shooting going on as we were ministering to the wounded. I was standing next to a rubber tree when I heard bullets hitting the tree. I got down on the ground and I could literally see blades of grass being chopped off next to me. I followed the tracers back to their source and was actually able to see the enemy soldier who was firing at us from up in a tree. I could tell that he was aiming at our wounded and those that were working on them. There was a rifle lying on the ground near me and I was tempted to pick it up to return fire, but thought better of it. I was a non-combatant and it would have been a violation of the Geneva Convention.

In the early stage of the battle, with enemy fire coming in from three different directions, an unarmed John Talley fully expected that he would not survive the day. But as he reported in our interview, he was ready. He knew where he was going, and it was ok.

The tracers that the Viet Cong and North Vietnamese forces used were white and greenish-white. Some Blue Spaders identified them as green and others as white. Our tracers were red. The advantage of using tracers is that the shooter is able to see where his shots are impacting without looking through the rifle's sights. It helps when a weapon is being fired from the hip or on full automatic or whenever one desires to maintain a full range of view in the target area. Looking through a gun's sights forces the shooter to focus on one small area. A major disadvantage of using tracers is that it gives the shooter's position away, a problem if one is shooting from a concealed location.

Sgt. Harold Gilbert (positioned toward the middle of Charlie Company in the right column):

I saw white and green tracers coming down out of the trees to my front and left and tracers coming from our right flank running parallel to the ground. The tracers were coming out of the trees at different angles depending on how far away from them our guys were. Some were coming almost straight down as though they were shooting at our men who were directly under them. The tracers that were running horizontal were mostly coming from the jungle on our right flank, but a few were coming from the left. It was as though we were caught in a horseshoe. At first, most of their firing seemed to be directed toward the center of our formation, toward the company command group where Captain Tavernetti was with the radios. There were a lot of them up in the trees, fifteen to twenty, or more. They were tied in with ropes. Some of them would swing out firing and then swing back into the tree tops. Some of them were firing at me. At one point, impacting bullets were digging up the ground around me and I couldn't move. I actually saw two of them up in the trees which I fired at. They were NVA wearing pith helmets and had branches tied on for camouflage. I could see tracers coming down out of several other trees in the area but I couldn't actually see the shooters. I fired at them and at the source of the tracers coming from the jungle on my right. I kept firing until the tracers stopped. I think I had three clips left when the shooting was over [riflemen carried a double basic load of ammunition, eighteen magazines or "clips" with eighteen rounds each].

Staff Sgt. Ray "Tex" Calvert:

I was acting platoon sergeant for Charlie Company's 2nd platoon on November 7. I was positioned between the two columns. Before the beginning of the battle when we were ordered to hold in place, I was sitting on my steel pot and was leaning against a rubber tree. I had just opened a can of peaches and finished it and was about half asleep when I started hearing bullets going by. They were cracking and popping right near my head. I hit the ground and got my pot on. I saw a green tracer coming on a downward angle pass by me. Then I saw more green tracers, some of them coming pretty close. I remember hearing Lt. Carnes holler "They're in the trees!" There weren't any in the trees right by me, but some distance away toward my right front near the jungle I saw them. They were tied in the trees on ropes and they would swing out into the open lane between the rows and fire as they were swinging. When they swung back in they would grab a limb and you couldn't see them. You had to fire at them while they were swinging before they disappeared.

Pfc. Ken Gross:

After the intense firing of the initial stage of the ambush died down, some other Charlie company guys came forward to help us out. There was still enemy fire coming out of the trees and along the jungle. Some of our guys were engaging them while others were dragging our dead and wounded back to the main body of our intact lines. Since I wasn't hit I helped to drag our wounded. I saw that the platoon RTO was wounded so I took his radio and I became the platoon RTO at that point.

Sp4 Frank Kepple, Charlie Company, machine gunner:

I was in the 1st platoon walking in the left column. When the firing started I went right to the ground. After a few minutes when the intense firing had slackened down my gun squad was ordered forward. Bullets were still snapping around us and I didn't want to get up, but the four of us dashed forward and fortunately none of us got hit. Someone hollered "The trees! The trees! They're in the trees!" I just opened up with the gun firing into the surrounding trees. Not just me. Everyone in the area was firing into the trees and I saw three or four of them fall out.

Staff Sgt. Ray Calvert:

From my location, there were green tracers coming at us from four directions. A high volume of fire was coming out of the trees to my front, right where the lead elements of our column were; a small volume was coming down out of the trees to our left; there was fire coming from our right flank [from the edge of the jungle fifty to seventy-five meters away]; and there was fire coming from our rear [from Delta Company's location]. At that point in time [the first few minutes of the battle] we didn't know if it was enemy or friendly. That's when Captain Tavernetti came by and told me to go forward and get 3rd Platoon to quit shooting back at us. He thought that the lead platoon was shooting toward us responding to the shooting coming from our rear, but all I saw was green and white tracers. I didn't see any red tracers coming our way at all. Captain Tavernetti had probably never seen enemy tracers before. They had us almost completely pinned down at that point. As soon as the shooting died down some, I made a dash for the front, drawing fire as I went. I could see the tracers flying around me. I ran approximately fifty to sixty meters and dove to the ground amidst a heavy volume of fire. I slid in the last ten meters behind a rubber tree. Green and white tracers were coming out of the wood line just two rows of rubber trees to my right flank. Again, the shooting died down, but every time I moved they would open up on me.

I found myself in 3rd Squad's sector near the head of the right column. All of the squad was down, dead or wounded. There was nobody there that was able to fire. There was one guy who was in a sitting position leaning against a rubber tree and he had been shot. I knew if he stayed upright like he was that he was going to get slaughtered. When I got to him he said he couldn't feel his legs. He had blood all over the front of his fatigue shirt and also had blood on his back. I figured a spinal wound. I had to make a decision on the spot either to lay him down and paralyze him permanently or leave him sitting up and get killed, so I laid him down. Fortunately he wasn't shot through the spine as far as I know, and later I found out that he did survive. As I was working on him trying to get a field dressing on his wounds I started receiving fire again. Bullets were impacting all around pinning me down. If I even lifted my head up above the grass, which was about the depth of my body, I was shot at. Some of the undergrowth around me had seed pods on them at the ends of the stems. As I lay there I was watching the pods get cut off by flying bullets and falling to the ground. I knew that whoever it was had me zeroed in. If I so much as twitched he opened up on me. At that point there was no fire from our formation near my location going out towards the jungle at all.

A short time later, as I was still pinned down there, the artillery Liaison Officer [Capt. Michael Cochran], and his RTO [Sp4 John Ensell] came forward and dove behind the same tree with me. The artillery officer was lying right next to me with his helmet even with my waist. Immediately, he went to work on the radio coordinating either the artillery or the air strikes. The RTO was behind me with the hand guard of his M16 resting on the calf of my leg. At that point we were taking fire primarily from one location in the jungle from the column's right flank, but I couldn't pinpoint exactly where it was coming from. Then the RTO said "I see him, I see him." When he fired a burst at the location in the bushes I was watching and saw where his tracers were hitting. When the enemy soldier returned fire at us I saw the leaves blow apart from the muzzle blast of his AK-47. So then I emptied a whole magazine at the spot on full automatic and so did the RTO. After that it was quiet from that area.

At the end of the battle when this location was being secured, Calvert checked out the area and found the body of a young soldier wearing a green uniform (NVA) with several bullet wounds in his torso. Next to him was an AK47 with twelve rounds remaining in the clip. Two other empty magazines were at his side. Ray noted that the AK was brand new and still had packing grease on it. Also, it was shortly after this action that the liaison officer and his RTO, were killed and a severely wounded Captain Dobbins took over coordination of artillery support.

It was just a few minutes later that our senior aid man, Szydlowski, came strolling up through there like it was a Sunday picnic. I said to him, "Man you better get your tail down." Fortunately, by that time we had stopped taking fire in our area. There was still shooting going on back behind us, but not right where we were.

Sp5 Ralph Szydlowski:

It wasn't long after we moved out from the village that I remember all of a sudden the column started running like they were chasing something. I was between the two columns right at the point where the formation was turning left. Then I heard First Sergeant Poolaw, who was a little way behind me at the back of Charlie Company, hollering to slow down or stop. I think the Captain [Tavernetti] was also yelling to stop. That's when I first heard some firing. It was quite a distance away, just a couple of pops. Then I remember Poolaw shouting, 'Hit the ground!' Then the shooting started. The first call for medic that I heard was Stoltenow [Pfc. Ronald Stoltenow, who was also one of Charlie Company's medics]. He was shot in the gut; I got an I.V. going on him and heard a single shot to my right. I looked across through the brush just as another shot rang out and I saw Poolaw get hit. He was just twenty-five to thirty feet away. He was prone on the ground and just flopped over. When I got over there he was dead. There was another man next to him and he was shot in the butt. It was a clean wound; the bullet had passed right through one of the cheeks. I was putting a dressing on him when a couple of rounds came in on us. It seemed like they were coming from the trees. The guy I was working on had lost his rifle so I grabbed Poolaw's but it was empty. I loaded it and fired off a clip, reloaded it and gave it to him. After I finished bandaging him up I went forward because that's where most of the company was located. Near the front I found the artillery FO and his RTO. He was trying to help a guy with a sucking chest wound. I put an I.V. on him, patched him up and then moved farther on up where I came upon a machine gun squad. They were all down, dead [Actually, machine gunner, Charlie White was still alive, but may have been unconscious or appeared dead with a terrible head/facial wound and gunshot wound to his hip]. I checked their gun and found that it was inoperable. I didn't see any more of our casualties up front so I came back in and I saw one of Captain Tavernetti's RTOs with an open gut wound. He must have been grazed and it opened him right up, so I started taking care of him. Then I saw Faircloth [medic, James Faircloth] laying on the ground and I yelled at him to get up. I didn't know at the time that he had been hit. He was laying there with a real peaceful look and he was holding a little black Bible. He had a gut wound. Just beyond Faircloth there was a group of wounded where I found Captain Tavernetti. He was being taken care of by the second platoon medic [Pfc. Dennis Collins] who had moved forward. He had already put him on an IV and was bandaging his wounds. Tavernetti's other wounded RTO was also there and one other wounded soldier.

Sp4 Bernie Jaworowski, Charlie Company, rifleman, 2nd Platoon:

After about twenty minutes to one-half hour the shooting slackened to sporadic fire from the trees and jungle but there was still considerable firing going on in Delta Company's sector, automatic fire and explosions. When the shooting stopped completely I, and others as well, got up to check out the situation and take inventory of our men. As I was walking around I bumped into Billy Joe Barnett who was lying on his back in the underbrush. My foot hit his leg. Billy winced and I apologized, but I could tell that he was in tough shape. Billy was a real nice guy; soft-spoken with a southern accent. He was still alive when we got him to the medevac, but died of his wounds sometime later.

CHAPTER 9

Delta Company's Sector

Capt. Ray Dobbins, Delta Company, commander:

After the search of the village was complete we headed east through the rubber moving parallel to the southern edge of the plantation. My right column was a few rows in from the edge of the rubber. The artillery guys were walking their 105s along with us, having them fire a round every five minutes or so and adjusting them as we moved.

A problem we ran into at that time involved our flankers on the right side of the column. They were walking just beyond the rubber in the jungle. They had a radio and they were reporting that they were seeing people in green uniforms with helmets on. This happened a couple of times on one of the previous day's patrols and they turned out to be the lead company's clover leafs coming back into the column in our sector, but this time they were having difficulty identifying friend from foe. I was on my way out there to check it out when I saw several uniformed men coming out of the jungle and into the rubber. They had their helmets camouflaged with leaves, but they were some distance away and I couldn't tell right away if they were NVA. That's when all hell broke loose. They were up moving and attacking our column. It was at this same time when the battalion command group got hit. LTC Stigall and the others were about twenty-five meters in front of me at the time. RPGs were coming in real heavy around them and then around us. They hit our formation with RPGs first before they ever fired a single round from an AK-47 or a machine gun. My RTO took a direct hit on his radio and the same blast hit me [shrapnel wound in the neck] and took out my other RTO as well. So both my RTOs were down and both radios were out. It seemed as though the North Vietnamese were targeting anyone carrying a radio or anyone close to a radio. In those first few minutes of the battle if you were close to a radio in their range you were dead or wounded. It was just that simple. And that's why we lost the command group.

Staff Sgt. Billy Collins, Delta Company, acting platoon sergeant:

Shortly after we heard the individual shots fired toward the front of Charlie

Company we heard them getting hit with multiple explosions, and then we got hit from our right flank. All hell was breaking loose. There was shooting everywhere. We were in the rubber about fifty meters from the tree line and I saw twenty to thirty of them coming out of the jungle. They had camouflage in their helmets and tied all over their bodies and they were moving from tree to tree coming toward us. Captain Dobbins and his two RTOs had been hit but he was still able to remain in control and he told me that we had to get everybody on line and get the guns working [M60 machine guns].

Back at the NDP, acting platoon sergeant Staff Sgt. Larry Van Lancker and his RTO from Delta Company's 2nd Platoon were monitoring the company radio net. His platoon was the one that was back at the NDP because they were scheduled for ambush patrol that night.

Staff Sgt. Larry Van Lancker, Delta Company:

We could hear the sounds of the battle over the radio and we heard individual soldiers yelling out the locations of enemy so that our guys could direct their fire on them. I heard Dobbins yelling that a group of enemy was close to the battalion command post [which would have been just a short distance ahead of Dobbin's position]. And I was listening when CPT Dobbins got hit.

Pfc. Jim Murray, Delta Company, 1st Platoon, rifleman:

On November 7, I was at the front of Delta Company's left column. The battalion command group was just a short distance ahead of me. LTC Stigall was just 40 feet or so to my right front. When the shooting started I hit the ground immediately. It seemed like the shooting was coming from everywhere, but then I realized it was coming mainly from the jungle to my front and from the jungle on my right flank. I was completely pinned down for a long while. Every time I tried to move . . . just raise my head to look around, bullets would come in on me, hitting the tree next to me or hit the ground along side of me. One of the times that I did raise myself up I saw that the Colonel had been hit. He was lying on his back and someone was working on him, but I could tell it was bad. I could hear him barking out orders, but it was like he was delirious because what he was saying didn't make sense. A few minutes later I saw that he was by himself and appeared to be dead.

Sometime after this, an already dead Lt. Col. Stigall was again struck by an enemy bullet leaving a massive head wound. When I got to his location with the relief force we identified his body by the cast on his foot and his name tag.

Sgt. Klem Kaniho, Delta Company, 1st Platoon, squad leader:

I was in the lead squad in the left column when all hell broke loose up front of us and we really didn't know what was happening up there. Then RPGs started coming in on us and I got hit with a piece of shrapnel in my arm. Right from the beginning there were guys calling for medics mixed in with the sounds of automatic weapons fire and RPG blasts.

Platoon Sgt. Tom Hicks, Delta Company, 1st Platoon:

Our platoon had the left column on November 7. My RTO had the long, "whip" antenna on the radio that day [for better and longer range radio transmission capability]. Shortly after the beginning of the battle we could hear bullets cracking over our heads and he said to me "Sarge, they're shooting at you!" I said, "No. They're shooting at you and your radio! Switch to your short antenna." Also, early on, I remember third platoon hollering "Wounded coming through!" The guys in the right column were bringing the wounded back away from the enemy fire coming out of the jungle.

Sgt. Ed Kleinschmit, Delta Company, squad leader:

My squad was bringing up the rear of the left column on November 7. We were spread out pretty far in the rubber. I remember that we were stopped and I was getting out some C-rations to grab a bite to eat when all kinds of firing and explosions opened up to our front in the area of the battalion command group and then to our right flank. Our right column was firing, but I didn't want to fire over our own men so I held fire until I actually had some definite targets. Later, we moved over to join the right column. There was a lot of tall grass in our area and the guys said to fire at places where the grass was moving as the VC had come out of the jungle and had been crawling toward our position. Our artillery was flashing all around us and we got flat on the ground behind trees to try to avoid getting hit by our own stuff. After the artillery fire stopped helicopter gunships strafed the jungle all along the edge of the rubber.

Sgt. Eddie Dumas, Delta Company, 1st Platoon, squad leader:

I was walking in the left column on November 7. When the battle opened up I hit the dirt. There was fire coming at us from the jungle to our right. The grass was knee deep where I was and I wasn't able to see well enough from the ground to locate any targets or to avoid hitting our guys that were in the right column so I stood up behind a rubber tree so I could see where I was shooting. AK 47 rounds were coming close to me. I could hear bullets zinging through the air and I was returning fire back into the jungle. For a time, one of them had me zeroed in, but as long as I was standing sideways behind the tree all he did was chip bark off the tree. Well, in order to shoot I had to expose part of my right side, so I would lean out just far enough to raise my M16 to get a burst off. One time as I was leaning out to shoot a bullet passed right through my mustache and it must have been a tracer because I could smell the hair burning.

The North Vietnamese forces that the Blue Spaders ran into on November 7 were well disciplined. The individuals that were positioned in trees and those hidden in the jungle brush along both legs of their position were apparently instructed to hold their fire until the ambush was initiated with a barrage of rocket propelled grenade fire. The NVA that were in the trees held their fire even after two of their men had been detected by Charlie Company's lead element and were taken under fire. The NVA that were seen moving toward the formation by Delta Company's flankers did not open fire when they were observed (it is possible that they may not have known that they had been detected). The fact that they were not in a fixed position as were those in the trees or those along Charlie Company's right flank and Delta Company's forward right flank is an indication that the ambushers were reacting to the situation as it developed. They had a large enough force that they were able to maneuver a sizable contingent of their men to attack and try to penetrate through Delta Company's column. Had they been successful they would have been able to attack Charlie Company's unprotected rear and encircle the divided column. Annihilation of the Blue Spaders would have been a possibility. Their attempt to take out the battalion's leaders and radiomen fell just short of its goal. It was a wounded Capt. Ray Dobbins and his ability to bring the artillery to bear after the forward observers were killed and C Company commander Capt. Len Tavernetti was put out of commission that saved the day.

Capt. Ray Dobbins:

> The attacking NVA were between me and my flank. My flankers were cut off and I didn't know at that point if they were dead or alive. I do know that at least two of them were killed at some point. I brought the platoon from our left column over and had them get on line with our right column so they could face the attacking NVA. Some of our men were coming right through the battalion command group's location so I had them pick up a radio with the battalion radio frequency on it. With the battalion radio and one that they had, I had my two radios back.
>
> Next, I knew we had to get our artillery going. The battalion forward observer had been knocked out with LTC Stigall and the rest of the command group. We got a hold of his radio and I was able to establish contact with the battalion's artillery liaison officer who was with Charlie Company's command group. He had the artillery working along Charlie Company's right flank and then I got it going along our [Delta Company's] right flank. It was busting in the jungle and in the rubber right up to our positions. You could see the enemy bodies flying all over the place in the artillery blasts. I was afraid that we would take casualties from our own ordnance, but it was where we needed it. They were that close. During that time someone up the chain of command tried to have them check fired [stop firing] so that helicopter gunships could come in. I protested because I had the artillery working right where I wanted it. There were helicopters in depth in the air above the battle. Battalion, brigade, and division level staff were monitoring the action and we were getting all kinds of requests to pop smoke. We were ignoring most of it because what's the reason to pop smoke? All that does is let them [the brass up in the helicopters flying over the battle] know where you are at. Finally, General Coleman [Assistant Division Cmdr. William S. Coleman] gave orders for all the helicopters to clear out of the area and to clear the [radio] net. That was a big help because it allowed me to focus on what needed to be done without having to deal with everybody else that was talking. I went through about six radio operators that day because every time anybody picked up a radio he got hit.
>
> The artillery broke their back. It forced them to break contact and withdraw. I understand that we had artillery from two fire bases firing that day. General Coleman told me later that he had everything going that could reach us [A Battery 6/15 Artillery and B Battery 2/33 Artillery].

After we had the artillery working I called Charlie 6 [C Company Cmdr. Len Tavernetti] and he said that he was hit and couldn't move. I was looking for someone to take over the battalion because Dobol 6 [Battalion Commander, Lieutenant Colonel Stigall] was dead. Tavernetti out ranked me so he should have been the one to take over. I told him that I was hit but still mobile so I would take over the Battalion. At that time I put Lieutenant Karl in charge of Delta Company, he was the only commissioned officer that I had out there, and I told Tavernetti that I needed somebody in charge of Charlie Company. He told me that he didn't have anybody. So I started walking up toward their position. I passed through the Battalion Command Group and saw that they were all dead. I passed several more dead and wounded before I found where CPT Tavernetti was. By this time a small group was gathered around him. I saw that there were a couple of platoon leaders there so I told them that I needed one of them to take over the Company [see appendix 3 for Len Tavernetti's experience after November 7].

Sgt. G. B. Gastor, Charlie Company:

Within half an hour or so the jets started to come in and they were close. They were dropping napalm at tree top level and firing 20mm canon. You could see the fireballs from the napalm at the edge of the jungle. Butterfly bombs also. You could see them coming down, so we moved back a short distance away from the jungle. After the jets came through it was pretty much over. At that point we moved back further and into the main column. That's where I saw First Sergeant Poolaw dead with the back of his head blown off. I took his fatigue shirt and pulled it up and put it over his head. Near there I saw the chaplain and some others helping with the wounded. Captain Tavernetti was there lying on his back and they were working on him. At that point I started helping with the wounded also. Then I went around the area trying to account for our guys.

Sp5 Ralph Szydlowski, Charlie Company, senior medic:

Some time after I had come back into Charlie Company's CP area and was checking on all our wounded, a runner from Delta Company came forward and said that they had been hit bad. I headed back toward Delta Company. At the back of Charlie Company I found one of Delta Company's medics working on one of our men. Both his legs were shot all to hell so I assisted him. He had started an I.V. and it was almost dry so he was looking for more fluid to put in him. I didn't have any so I told him to try to get him to drink some water. I left him and there was a gap between Charlie Company's rear and Delta Company's position. When I got there I found their senior medic and he had their wounded arranged in a horseshoe. He was working on them but had the situation under control. He said the other casualties were all dead.

At this point Delta's senior medic was unaware of other wounded that were positioned some distance away from his location. The undergrowth in the rubber trees in the battle area varied from very sparse, low grass to relatively thick grass and weeds up to three feet high. In Delta Company's sector the undergrowth was taller and thicker than much of the undergrowth in Charlie Company's sector. Short of a thorough search of the area, which was not completed until the relief column arrived some time later, it was not possible to know the extent of the casualties. If wounded men were not crying out for help, which some were reluctant to do in light of the closeness of the enemy, their existence would not have been apparent to anyone at the time of Szydlowski's visit.

Charlie Company's senior medic was out of medical supplies at this point except for one dressing and morphine. He lamented the fact that he was required to carry an M16 and its complement basic load of ammunition. He would have preferred to carry extra medical supplies. He noted that one of the Company's medics, Pfc. Dennis Collins, was a C.O. [conscientious objector] and that most of the men did not want him to be their medic due to his refusal to carry any kind of weapon.

Sp5 Ralph Szydlowski:

> I think we [medics] all were C.O.s after November 7. If I needed a weapon I could have picked one up. If I was doing my job somebody was already hit and I could always use their weapon. I carried three of them out of there that day. What got me was that I ran out of equipment. When Alpha Company came out with the battalion surgeon they came with a lot of supplies, but by then it was pretty much too late. For the next couple of months I refused to carry a weapon and I was finally told, "OK, you can carry a .45 if you want it," so I started carrying a .45 pistol.

Capt. Ray Dobbins:

> We were fortunate that the artillery worked as well as it did because it basically turned the tide and the enemy withdrew. I told Lt. Karl to move Delta Company up and secure a landing zone so we could start getting our wounded and dead out. He moved both of Delta Company's platoons up to an area just to our North. I called up to the battalion LOH [light observation helicopter] to see if he could land in the NDP and pick up our chain saws. He came back out and dropped the saws down in a basket and our guys went to work felling rubber trees.

The effort to clear an LZ in the rubber had to be abandoned when the chain saws clogged with rubber sap and quickly became inoperable. General Coleman wanted Maj. Gene Luthultz, battalion executive officer, who was in the LOH, to take command of the battalion. It was safer for Major Luthultz to land in the chopper, but without a secure area to land near the battalion he had to go back to the NDP and march out with the relief force (Alpha Company).

Captain Dobbins had informed General Coleman that the enemy had broken contact and that the immediate area had been secured. He discussed with him the need to have the relief force sweep the battle area. When Alpha Company got to the battle site we went immediately to locating and securing a landing zone for the medevacs and then carrying the casualties to the evacuation point. No organized sweep of the battle area was ever initiated, no body count was made, no documents were recovered, and a relatively low number of enemy weapons were recovered. It wouldn't have taken much time to conduct a sweep, but for unknown reasons it was never accomplished.

CHAPTER 10

The Big Tree

SEVERAL OF THE MEN that were near the middle of the formation mentioned that there was a large tree at the edge of the jungle on the right flank. It became a point of reference for the helicopter and jet fighter pilots as they made their strafing and bombing runs on the enemy positions. The tree stood out from the surrounding jungle because of its size, but also because the vegetation in the immediate area was mostly low scrub. The terrain features provided a clear line of demarcation for the pilots so they were able to put their ordnance on the enemy at the edge of the jungle and very close to the Blue Spader lines. One of the tactics that the enemy sometimes used in larger sized battles was to leave snipers behind to continue to fire upon their enemy in order to prevent the organization of a pursuing force. If they were dragging off their dead and wounded their trails would have been relatively easy to follow and their supplies of ammunition would have been depleted making them highly vulnerable. The arrival of the jets and gunships caused the remaining enemy to break contact.

Sp4 Bernie Jaworowski, Charlie Company:

I was a rifleman in the second platoon walking in the right column approximately in the middle of Charlie Company's formation. When the enemy opened up on us I dove to the ground and hit my chest on an eight-inch log, fracturing a couple of ribs. With the flow of adrenaline I was oblivious to the pain and didn't find out till later that they were broken. We were two or three rubber tree rows from the edge of the jungle and had just made the 90 degree turn to the left. The volume of fire was to a degree that I had never experienced before. There were green tracers coming from several directions. They were coming down from the rubber trees and from the jungle on our right flank. I was firing back up into the trees to my front and then along my right when I noticed that there were half a dozen enemy firing from a large tree at the edge of the jungle. Later, when the air support started to come in I shouted the information to a platoon leader from one of the other platoons that was near me and he radioed it in to whoever was in contact with the Air Force. When the first strafing run of an F-4 Phantom came in focused on the big tree they all just started dropping to the ground. I saw one hit the ground and immediately pop up and take off running. The Phantom made one more strafing run and then dropped a bomb on the tree.

Sp4 Harold Hughes, Charlie Company, radio telephone operator (RTO):

Where I was [between the two column formation] most of the enemy fire was coming from the trees. After some time when they were starting to bring in the artillery we were moved back to our left away from the jungle. When the air strikes came in there were "Cong" falling out of trees. Some were dead, hit by the jets' cannon fire and some hit the ground running. Our guys opened up on them and were cutting them down.

Sgt. Harold Gilbert:

The Phantoms brought napalm in very close, right at the edge of the jungle. You could feel the heat off the napalm. It was just like opening an oven door the way the heat came in on us. We didn't have any smoke. They had called for us to pass up our smoke grenades earlier so they could mark our position. We were just hoping they wouldn't drop it on us.

Butch Gearing was the senior NCO for Charlie Company since First Sergeant Poolaw was dead. He began accounting for the company's men even before the relief force arrived. He and his RTO ranged out into the area where some of the most intense fighting had occurred at the head of Charlie Company's right flank and up to the edge of the jungle.

Staff Sgt. Butch Gearing:

When we rejoined the column we filled in the area of the Company's forward right flank. The shooting had died way down and we could move around. There were a lot of dead enemy on the ground beyond our position, twenty or more. Some had black clothing and others were wearing green. Some of them had pith helmets. [Viet Cong generally wore black pajama-like clothing and North Vietnamese regulars generally wore green or khaki uniforms and soft, full brimmed shade hats or pith helmets.]

Sgt. Greer Cappello, Charlie Company:

Near the end of the battle I saw one NVA soldier appear at the edge of the jungle. There was very little shooting going on at this point. He wasn't firing at me so I just let him go and watched him. He had a two-wheel cart and didn't appear to have a weapon. I watched as he picked up a dead comrade, placed him on the cart, and then disappear back into the jungle.

CHAPTER 11

The Relief Force

At the first hint of trouble Alpha Company commander, James Altmeyer, alerted the Company to "saddle up" and stand ready to move out even before radio contact had been reestablished with the battalion. Meanwhile, the Blue Spaders' executive officer, Gene Luthultz, who was now the battalion's ranking officer, arrived at the NDP by helicopter. When radio contact was restored Major Luthultz marched out with the relief force to take command of the battalion.

Pfc. Thomas Dombek, Alpha Company, rifleman:

On the morning of November 7 my platoon was on a patrol outside the battalion perimeter. We got word that Charlie and Delta had been ambushed and that we were to double time it back to the perimeter to join the relief force. When we got back our whole Company pulled out. I was put on the right flank with two other guys from my platoon. They gave us a radio and sent us out about a hundred meters from the main column. It was unusual because it was the first time I had ever had a radio on flank security, and normally we would go out only about 30 meters. The fighting was over by the time we arrived at the battle site. I came through some brush and tripped on a dead GI. He was lying on his back with his eyes open looking up at me. Most of our guys were deployed to secure the area. I was assigned to the task of carrying the dead to the evacuation point.

Sp4 Roger Boling, Alpha Company, rifleman:

I remember that November 7 was the first break that Alpha Company had in a long time. We got to stay back and work on the bunkers and perimeter, but basically we had the day off. When we got word that the battalion patrol got caught in an ambush I remember that I could hear the sounds of the battle off in the distance. On the way out there we were looking for snipers in trees and as we got to the battle site the first thing that I saw was a dead enemy hanging in a rubber tree. It looked like he was caught by his foot. While I was out there I saw a few other enemy bodies that were on the ground. They had uniforms on, not black pajamas. They were NVA. Some of our platoon were assigned to secure the area, but I was assigned to carry bodies. One of the bodies that I carried out [with the author] was the colonel. [Asked if he remembered the head wound that Lieutenant Colonel Stigall had sustained, Boling said that he did not.] I knew it was the colonel by the cast on his foot and the insignia on his uniform. I must have blocked it out.

When the relief force reached the battle site the area was secured, and as noted previously, the effort to clear a landing zone for the medevac choppers was initiated. Chain saws were brought out by helicopter and lowered through the overhead canopy. Alpha Company soldiers went right to work attempting to cut rubber trees, but quickly learned a hard lesson. You can't bring down live rubber trees with chain saws. The thick, heavy sap clogs up the drive sprockets and chains and renders them useless. An alternate site outside the perimeter would have to be found. Meanwhile, surviving NCOs went about the work of accounting for their men. A small clearing was soon located not too far from the edge of the rubber that would allow a single chopper to land at a time. The area was secured and the casualties were carried to the site. A surgical team from one of the other units operating in the area (led by Capt. Samuel L. Kalush, 1st Battalion, 28th Infantry) was choppered in and the work of treating and evacuating the wounded began expeditiously.

Sp4 Charlie White, Charlie Company:

Everyone around me was down, dead or wounded. I remember feeling my wounds [shrapnel to the side of his face and a bullet in his right hip] and thinking that if I didn't bleed to death that I would probably survive. There were bomb explosions going off really close and dirt was falling down on top of me, but all I could do was lie there and wait. It seemed like a long time before a medic came forward. He put a bandage on my hip and said that somebody would be up soon to get me. When the guys came up to take me out they put me on one of those roll up stretchers and it hurt so bad that I told them to put me down and leave me alone. The pain was unbearable. Fortunately, they weren't taking orders from me and continued carrying me to the evacuation point. They set me down with several of the other wounded and next to First Sergeant Poolaw. He was dead.

I remember talking to Butch Gearing while I was there. He asked me if I wanted him to get my hymn book out and sing me a hymn. I used to carry a hymn book that the chaplain had given us during a field service. I used to like to sing those hymns to myself. A short time after that, I was evacuated. I remember being glad to be on that helicopter getting out of there.

Pfc. Thomas Dombek, with Alpha Company on the relief force (Response after he was asked if he saw any signs of the enemy in the battle area):

While I was in the area I saw two dead VC. One was up in a rubber tree. He had been tied in and was slumped over the rope that held him in place. The other one was in a foxhole partially covered with brush. Also in the area, I saw two AK47s that someone had picked up and leaned against a tree.

CHAPTER 12

"Greater Love Hath
No Man Than This . . ."*

I‌T WASN'T UNTIL THAT FIRST REUNION IN CHICAGO in June of 2001 that I found out that one of the Blue Spaders killed on November 7 had received the Medal of Honor.

In the initial stage of the battle, the firing was intense at the head of Charlie Company's right column. The 3rd Platoon's 3rd Squad, seven men strong, found themselves fighting for their lives with RPG and automatic weapons fire pouring out of the tree line just a short distance away along their right flank. Their situation was made worse by numerous NVA positioned up in the trees and firing down on them from above. The squad's point man, Sp4 Robert Stryker, who carried a grenade launcher, was wounded in the initial volley of enemy fire (reportedly a bullet wound to one of his hands). Disregarding his wound and the enemy fusillade, Stryker returned fire launching grenades into the jungle to the column's right and into the surrounding rubber trees. With most of his squad down, dead or wounded, he spotted three enemy at the edge of the jungle setting up a large Claymore mine on a tripod aimed at the area where Jim Faircloth, 3rd Platoon medic, was working on Ron Payne and other 3rd Squad casualties. (While working on Payne, Faircloth was hit in the arm. He bandaged himself up and continued to work on the severely wounded Payne before he was again struck by a bullet to his midsection, the effects of which soon took him out of commission). It is unknown why Stryker did not fire on the Claymore team. Possibly, he feared that the blast from a grenade might set off their mine. He charged the enemy position and was just a few feet from it when it was detonated. Stryker's body absorbed much of the blast, shielding his wounded comrades. Later it was reported by others who had observed his body that there wasn't a square inch of his front torso that wasn't pierced with shrap-nel. Sp4 Bob Morris, who carried Stryker's M79 back to the NDP that night,

---

* *Greater love hath no man than this, that a man lay down his life for his friends.*
(JOHN 15:13, THE HOLY BIBLE, KJV)

reported that it too bore shrapnel scars from the Claymore blast.

Pfc. Ken Gross, Charlie Company:

On the 7th of November, I was an RTO and had only been in country a couple of months. I was with our squad leader at the front of the second squad in the right column walking 20–30 yards behind Stryker when all hell broke loose. We were in their kill zone. Half of the guys up forward of me were hit before they could get to the ground. It seemed like fire was coming from everywhere. Within seconds everyone forward of me was dead or wounded. In the first few minutes my radio was knocked out by an RPG blast. White tracers were coming down at us from the trees and others were running parallel to the ground, coming out of the dense jungle to our right flank. Initially, I was just basically firing my M16 back at the source of the tracers. At one point I actually saw two enemy that were up in the rubber trees [Gross took them both out].

A short time after that four of them came out of the jungle line running at us. They got pretty close before we were able to cut them down. Then I saw Stryker, still within minutes of the start of the battle, pop up and charge toward the jungle. A big Claymore exploded at the edge of the tree line. He was within five yards of the thing when it went off. The blast hit him hard and he was thrown backwards to the ground. I knew that he was gone.

When the shooting had stopped and the relief forced had arrived, the area was secured. After the effort to clear a landing zone within the secure perimeter in the rubber trees failed and the alternate site was located, the task of removing the dead and wounded got underway. The LZ for the medevacs was located not too far from the edge of the rubber plantation, but it required carrying the casualties some distance.

Sp4 Bernie Jaworowski, Charlie Company:

After carrying Billy Joe Barnett to the evacuation point, [George] Martinez and I carried out Stryker. We found his body about 75 meters to our right front, still in the rubber but close to the edge of the jungle. There were no other dead or wounded in the area near him. He was face down with his jungle uniform soaked with blood and there was no breathing. Since he was dead, we grabbed hold of his web gear and dragged him. He was face down and I was on his left side and Martinez was on his right. As we were dragging him, Stryker's left arm came around and wrapped around my right leg like he was grabbing me. It really spooked me and I thought that he must be alive. We stopped to check him out, but again there was no breathing and he was clearly dead.

In interviewing Charlie Company members, more than one expressed the idea that Bob Stryker was not a man you would have predicted to earn our nation's highest award for valor. The attitude he displayed was the antithesis of what you might call straight laced or "gung-ho" but his irreverent exterior obviously masked the fact that he cared deeply for his comrades in arms. He was not afraid to face grave personal danger. He did so willingly, even to the point of sacrificing his own life that his friends might live. His display of valor, above and beyond the call of duty, certainly does rank him among the greatest of our country's military heroes.

CHAPTER 13

Stryker and Poolaw

SEVERAL OF CHARLIE COMPANY'S MEMBERS commented on the special relationship that existed between Stryker and Poolaw. First Sergeant Pascal Poolaw in 1967 was a living legend. Like Lieutenant Colonel Stigall, Poolaw wore the Combat Infantryman Badge with two stars. Also, he had Purple Hearts from World War II and Korea. A full blooded Kiowa Indian, Poolaw had earned decorations for valor thirteen times in three wars. Poolaw loved his men, and his men loved him. Stryker had been in the Army for four or five years and had spent three years in Germany before coming to Vietnam. Normally, his rank should have been E-5 or E-6, instead of E-4 as it was on the November 7. The reason is that Stryker had a tendency to get himself into trouble and had a number of reductions in rank. His older brother, Jack Stryker, noted that Robert had reenlisted once, but really didn't like the army. According to his memory, in the fall of 1967 his brother was looking forward to getting out of the service.

As his platoon sergeant, Butch Gearing, notes below, Stryker was a good soldier. He had been given the responsibility of being a point man. Being on point requires some special characteristics and abilities. It is the position of greatest peril for an infantryman. He is the one out front blazing a trail. It requires unwavering vigilance. The point man must be watchful for signs of enemy presence and be able to handle the stress that the constant danger puts upon him. It's not a job entrusted to the faint of heart or to slackers. The point man commands the respect of all who follow behind. Stryker never got himself into trouble for anything he did out in the field. It was in the relatively less structured times at base camp when he sometimes ran afoul of the rules.

Sp4 Bob Morris:

> First Sergeant Poolaw and Robert Stryker were like two cats going after each other off and on. Stryker had the ability to make Poolaw mad and Poolaw would threaten to catch him and tar and feather him. It was funny to watch . . . as long as we all stayed out of their little battles.

Sp4 Bernie Jaworowski:

I remember one incident when Stryker had gotten in trouble and top ["top" Sergeant Poolaw] hollered "Stryker!" and then chewed him out for something. Even though he was in trouble you could tell that there was some kind of mutual bond between them.

Stryker was kind of a loner. Several Charlie Company soldiers told me that he tended to keep himself somewhat aloof. He used to keep others at arm's length by directing a somewhat more vulgar version of "Your mother wears combat boots!" at them. It appears in retrospect that this may have been an effort by Stryker to protect himself from the emotional consequences should he suffer the loss of any of those close to him.

Wreathea O'Hara, classmate and friend:

Robert tended to portray a hard shell to others. He wouldn't back down when confronted by others [at school]. But under that shell was a soft and caring heart.

Staff Sgt. Butch Gearing:

Stryker was a good soldier, but he wasn't the kind of guy who would give you instant obedience when you told him to do something, especially if he didn't see an obvious need for the task in question. Sometimes you had to stay on him. That's why I was surprised when I heard how he died.

Poolaw made it his pet project to keep Stryker in line, but I think Poolaw really liked Stryker. Poolaw was a father figure and he cared about all his men. The Company was really bummed out after losing Poolaw. We lost a lot of good guys, but the biggest loss was Poolaw.

Sp4 Bob Morris:

There were many a teary eyed grunt as we carried Poolaw's body to the evacuation point. Some of the men who knew him well were very upset. We had lost not only a good leader, but an inspirational one as well.

CHAPTER 14

Lessons Learned

IT HAS PROBABLY ALWAYS BEEN TRUE throughout the history of warfare that the number one goal when engaging an enemy is to do it on your terms and not his whenever possible. You want to have the advantage, and you want him to have the disadvantage. In Vietnam, our advantage was firepower—artillery and air. Artillery firebases were set up that could provide covering fire for all but the most remote of our ground operations. Air power included a wide variety of aircraft: helicopter gunships that can hover over a battle site and put machine gun and rocket fire close in to our troops on the ground; slow-flying, fixed-wing gunships that carry miniguns, multibarreled machine guns capable of putting out thousands of rounds of fire per minute and can blanket a wide area on the ground; jet fighters that can put napalm, antipersonnel bomblets (CBUs), 20mm cannon fire, large bombs with quick fuses for above-ground targets and delay fuses for below ground targets (bunkers and tunnels).

The Communists' advantage was concealment and surprise. They used the jungle and rubber plantation canopy to hide their base camps, movements, and fighting positions from the air. They were masters at camouflage and tunneling to conceal them from the ground and protect them from our firepower. The terrain was used to minimize our aerial surveillance and power. In line with this was their fundamental tactic in combat: "hold on to the Americans by the belt." In other words, to be so close as to render our artillery and air strikes useless.

It is true that hindsight is 20/20. It is also generally true that it takes aggressiveness to win battles and that too much caution accomplishes little on the field of combat. On November 7 a little more caution would probably have resulted in a better outcome. Another issue that came to bear was lack of experience. When fleeing VC were encountered, caution and experience might have dictated a different course: pull back, saturate the area of danger with artillery, then proceed.

Many in the battalion had never seen a North Vietnamese uniform before. If Delta Company's flankers had been able to identify the NVA as enemy when they first reported seeing them, they could have engaged them. Their firing would have put the whole formation on the ground before the ambush was blown. They would have been better able to withstand the RPG barrage and massive automatic weapons fusillade that opened the ambush while they were standing targets, obliterating the command group and Charlie Company's 3rd Squad at the front of the right column and devastating battalion and company RTOs.

With infantry officers splitting their yearlong tour in country between six months of combat duty and six months of off-line duty, the leadership often suffered from experience deficits at various levels. All of these factors came into play on November 7, particularly in that Blue Spaders had encountered enemy snipers tied up in trees as early as August 1966,[7] but leader turnover evidently insured that the experience never made it into either the unit's battle lore, or its training.

Training should have included the tactics the enemy tended to employ and how to identify them by the weapons they used and the clothing and uniforms they wore. Again, when flankers on Delta Company's right flank spotted uniformed soldiers moving toward the column just prior to the initiation of the ambush, they should have opened fire on them. Although it is true that there were problems on previous operations when the lead company's cloverleaf patrols were reentering the column in Delta's sector, the uniforms they wore and the weapons they carried clearly identified them as American. Also, there could have been some question as to whether the soldiers they were seeing were the Army of the Republic of Vietnam (ARVN—the South Vietnamese army). Sometimes we worked in proximity with them, although definitely not on this operation. Again, if training had been provided which included identification of all forces involved in the war this problem could have been minimized, the friend or foe decision could be made quickly, and the appropriate response made without having to call in for instructions. ARVN wore uniforms that were unmistakably different from the Communist Viet Cong and North Vietnamese regulars. Their helmets were different. They carried M-1 rifles and carbines and American grenade launchers, not AK47s and RPG launchers. The AKs and RPGs were distinctly enemy weapons. As Ray Dobbins reported, when his flankers called in about the uniformed individuals approaching the column, he was on his way out to check out the situation when "all hell broke loose."

The situation in the Loc Ninh area was not routine. With large numbers of VC and NVA known to be in the area and their major push to seize the Special Forces base in progress, caution should have been the rule. That should have included the use of firepower to blanket suspected enemy ambush sites prior to checking them out. There was ample evidence on the afternoon of November 7 that the probability of an ambush was very high. This was clearly seen by many

---

7. See Cantigny First Division Foundation, *Blue Spaders, the 26th Infantry Regiment, 1917–1967*, (Wheaton, Ill.: Cantigny First Division Foundation, 1996) 174.

that day, from seasoned enlisted men on the scene to Alpha Company's CO and others monitoring the radio back at the NDP. The appropriate firepower that gave us the advantage was not brought to bear early enough to ensure a major victory and avert the magnitude of the losses that we suffered (It is possible that the withholding of artillery fire when its use was clearly indicated just prior to the ambush was purposeful. A clue to this possibility was found in Chaplain John Talley's diary entry for November 6: "Moved to a new NDP . . . east of Loc Ninh. VC got out of the box—so we moved the box . . . Col Stigall told me 'We are the bait.'" If the Blue Spaders were the bait to try to get the enemy to engage, it would explain why artillery might have been withheld. Its use would have discouraged them from holding their positions and initiating combat. Instead of engaging they could have held their fire and melted away along their predetermined escape routes).

And were there no lessons learned from the major battle that occurred just three weeks earlier, October 17, at the battle of Ong Thanh? There another 1st Division battalion, the 2nd Battalion, 28th Infantry (Black Lions), was decimated (including the loss of its battalion commander) in an ambush of very similar character. (The enemy placed several of their men in tree tops in that ambush). One enemy in a tree might be an observer or a lone sniper, but two? Ambush![8] Before November 7 I had never heard reference to enemy making use of tree tops as a tactic. Our eyes were typically glued to ground level when searching for evidence of the enemy while on patrol.

Also, when enemy soldiers flee before an advancing patrol one has to consider that there are only two possibilities: These guys are trying to get out of harm's way, or they purposely want you to follow them. Either way, the best policy would have been to chase them with artillery, not pursue them on foot into a possible ambush. On the November 7, when the battalion first encountered the fleeing enemy after the search of the village, the decision not to follow as they fled straight into the jungle in front of the main column (when the battalion made the left hand ninety degree turn instead of continuing after them) was the correct one. Not to make use of the artillery to rake the area of danger before proceeding was the wrong one. Had the battalion not made the turn and continued straight into the jungle the Blue Spaders would most assuredly have been in greater peril. The enemy would probably have opened up as the lead elements of the double column approached the jungle. The two columns would have been subjected to withering enfilade fire from a probable dense concentration of enemy gunners at that location, the same enemy that had so devastated the battalion command group. The battalion's right column would also have been engaged by the enemy concealed in the jungle on their right flank, and the

---

8. For a detailed account of that battle and its connection to the fighting at Loc Ninh see David Maraniss, *They Marched Into Sunlight,* (New York: Simon and Schuster, 2003). The author was actually able to interview two of the enemy combatants of that battle, one of which was the Viet Cong regiment's commander. His book provides a rare and insightful account of the enemy's side of the story including their strategy and tactics.

battalion's left column would have been engaged by the enemy up in the rubber trees along what would have been their left flank.

On November 7 when the day's route of travel was planned and mapped out, a critical error in judgment was made. Traveling in the open along an area that affords concealment is problematic. Most ambushes occur when you are in the open and the enemy is hidden in some sort of cover that conceals their position and affords them unobserved avenues of escape. Traveling in the relative open of the rubber along the edge of the jungle was just the scenario the enemy wanted. A better plan would have been to have the main column travel in the rubber, but further away from the edge of the jungle. The jungle area could have been checked out with short recon patrols. Also, an alternative plan would have been to travel in the jungle. It would have been much slower, but would have put the Blue Spaders in a much better position to fight by avoiding the enemy's kill zone.

Another fact that bore heavily on the story of November 7 came to light in the interview with the battalion chaplain, Captain John Talley. He noted that there were no cloverleaf patrols conducted after the search of the village. He was concerned at the time because he knew of their importance as a tool for detecting ambushes. Talley kept a diary and he recorded a note in the diary the afternoon of the seventh, just prior to the ambush, "still no cloverleafs for security." Had cloverleaf patrols been conducted at the point when the fleeing enemy were spotted, and the decision was being debated as to whether the battalion should continue on its predetermined path straight into the jungle or make the ninety degree turn to the left, it could have greatly changed the outcome in our favor. The battalion had not yet fully entered the enemy kill zone. Cloverleafs moving out laterally from Charlie Company's left column may have put that patrol into the kill zone of the ambushers in the trees, but it is probable that the enemy would not have fired on them, and it is possible that the Blue Spader patrol would have detected them. The cloverleaf that would have gone out to the battalion's front would have put them right among the ambushers set up in the jungle at the southeast corner of the rubber with a very high likelihood of bumping into them. The cloverleaf that would have gone out to Delta Company's right flank would very likely have run into the NVA that were positioned at the edge of the jungle there or run into those maneuvering into position at that very moment to attack them. To conduct cloverleafs at this point in the mission would have been reasonable and prudent. For unknown reasons they were not utilized. Surely the men conducting the cloverleafs would have been in grave danger, and many would probably have become casualties, but they would have served their purpose for the success of the mission and saved more American lives.

Capt. Ray Dobbins:

One of the mistakes I made was that I didn't have the frequency for the artillery so that I could turn it into my radio. At times like that you don't reach down for a piece of paper with important frequencies written on it. You have got to have it up here [in your head] You could have it written on the radio, but my radio got blown up. So that wouldn't have helped me.

Lessons That Were Learned

by Paul F. Gorman

The generation of leaders that emerged in the United States Army post-Vietnam was well aware of the evils of the individual replacement system then in use, particularly that of limiting battalion command to six months (or less), and tolerating in-country rotation that removed soldiers from line units to fill rear echelon billets. These policies led to dangerous mediocrity on the battlefield, to formulary performances vice canny tactics, techniques, and procedures. Those leaders, when they rose to positions of responsibility from which they could dictate Army-wide policy—such as Generals DePuy and Starry, successive commanders of TRADOC [Training and Doctrine Command]—caused the Army to shift its focus from the rights and well-being of individuals to the cohesion and tactical effectiveness of units of the combat arms, and to abandon individual replacement in favor of rotation of line battalions.

Shortly before General DePuy passed away, he wrote to Gen. Colin Powell, then Chairman of the Joint Chiefs, a letter that included this reminder:

> All historically important armed forces have developed their own distinctive operational style. For example, historians agree that the Roman style of warfare fitted well the objectives of the Senate and the People of Rome. The Roman's habit of encamping at the ends of each day's operations, and then of connecting their camps with high speed roads, enhanced freedom of both operational and strategic maneuver. There was nothing casual about the Roman military style. The Roman commanders all understood it, and so did their adversaries. And the Romans almost always won.

> There is emerging a distinctive American style of war, a style that is essentially joint, drawing on the unique capabilities of each service via centralized planning and decentralized execution. This jointness, plus an amalgam of surprise, discriminate use of overwhelming force, high operating tempo, and exploitation of advanced technology, has led to a whole new order of military effectiveness . . .

General DePuy admitted that in 1966 he used troop units as "bait" to bring regiments of the 9th VC Division to battle along Route 13 and the Minh Thanh road. But when he did so, it was within a carefully concerted "counter-ambush" plan that employed deception, placed an armored cavalry unit in the van of the "bait," and backed it up by ready, massive joint fires and poised airmobile reinforcements. DePuy observed that these principles were in operation at the battles of AP Gu and Bau Bang in 1967. Of the battles of Ong Thanh and Srok Rung later in that year, he remarked that the 1st Division seemed to have forgotten the wisdom of the "cloverleaf," of finding the enemy with the smallest possible unit, and of inviting enemy attack at a time and place of our choosing.

Honor Roll

The United States Army
Battle of Srok Rung
November 7, 1967

IN ADDITION TO THE EIGHTEEN SOLDIERS of the 1st Infantry Division and the Vietnamese interpreter listed below who died on November 7, 1967, many were wounded. The number varies in different accounts from twenty-two to thirty. Because the Purple Heart records at the First Division Archives in Wheaton, Illinois, are incomplete, this honor roll is limited to those who were killed in action or died from their wounds. Certainly all who put their lives in harm's way for noble reasons are worthy of honor.

All true patriots know that freedom isn't free. The history of mankind is not one of liberty, but of tyranny. The founders of our nation understood that the yearning of every man's heart was for personal freedom, and our government was designed around the belief that that yearning was in our nature and that it came from God. It's what America stands for. The American fighting man gives up his personal freedom for a season in order to secure it for himself and for others, hoping to pick it up again when his time of service is completed. Those of us who returned from the battle alive have our reward—to again dwell in the land of liberty and pursue happiness as we see fit without an oppressive government managing our lives. But those who did make the ultimate sacrifice have Liberty's eternal, highest honor. Their names will be marked throughout the ages denoting that they gave their lives for freedom.

Honor Roll

Headquarters Company, 1st Battalion, 26th Infantry Regiment,
1st Infantry Division

Lt. Col. Arthur D. Stigall, Battalion Commander; Chase, Louisiana
Platoon Sgt. George D. Clayton, Battalion Intelligence NCO; Belmar, New Jersey
Sgt. Charles E. Long, RTO; Clanton, Alabama
Pfc. Ronald G. Stoltenow, Medic; Hankinson, North Dakota

C Company, 1st Battalion, 26th Infantry Regiment, 1st Infantry Division

1st Sgt. Pascal C. Poolaw, Apache, Oklahoma
Sp4 Robert F. Stryker, Grenadier; Auburn, New York
Pfc. Larry C. Banks, Rifleman/Ammo Bearer; Nashville, Indiana
Sp4 Billie Joe Barnett, Jr., Rifleman; Overland, Missouri
Sgt. Ronald H. Payne, Squad Leader; Bloomingdale, Georgia
Sp4 John E. Young, Assistant Machine Gunner; Oconto, Wisconsin

D Company, 1st Battalion, 26th Infantry Regiment, 1st Infantry Division

Sp4 Lawrence W. Barkley, RTO; Columbus, Ohio
Sp4 James R. Brown, Rifleman; Tennessee Colony, Texas
Pfc. Walter C. Bunyea, Rifleman; Las Cruces, New Mexico
Sp4 Clarence L. Shaw, Rifleman; Ardmore, Oklahoma
Sp4 Larry E. Turner, Grenadier; Columbus, Ohio

B Battery, 1st Battalion, 5th Artillery Regiment, 1st Infantry Division

Capt. Michael D. Cochran, Liaison Officer; Lancaster, California
1st Lt. Terry A. Hendricks, Forward Observer, San Bernardino, California
Sp4 John R. Ensell, RTO, Steubenville, Ohio

Tin (last name unknown), Vietnamese Interpreter

Helicopter Pilot Paul Pelland's Experience at Loc Ninh—End of October 1967

EVIDENTLY THE INTELLIGENCE GUYS AT G-2 discovered that there was a large concentration of NVA units infiltrating south from Cambodia. Spoiling for a fight (Westmoreland was being pressured by higher-ups to get U.S. ground forces more involved, face-to-face with the enemy), it seemed like every unit of the 1st Division ended up at Quan Loi the first night. I remember sleeping on the bare floor of a 3/4 ton trailer that night.

I slept fitfully and was just getting into a real sleep when someone with a flashlight rousted me. I followed him into a dimly lighted TOC [tactical operations center] of the Infantry Battalion to which I was assigned for that time. Seems that a Special Forces compound located right next to the airstrip at Loc Ninh was under heavy attack. I was tasked to fly the Battalion Operations Officer to the camp there which was right up next to the Cambodian border. We took off in total darkness but with the hint of light of the false dawn off to our east, we headed north and west toward Loc Ninh with just the glow of the red instrument lights illuminating the night. Quan Loi artillery was shooting northwest providing blocking fire for the Loc Ninh situation so we had to fly parallel to the gun-target line. Almost there, I contacted the Special Forces and told them I was ten minutes out. The call sign for the Special Forces guys was "Gory Segment" which lent a scary undertone to the approaching dawn. He said they were under heavy attack from the north and that I was to land at the south end of the airstrip, next to the artillery battery gun pits. I was familiar with Loc Ninh as I visited there many times and had refueled at the south end of the airstrip, right where I was instructed to land. The artillery from Quan Loi was impacting in the rubber trees just north of the strip.

Landing was uneventful. All I had to do was to discharge the operations officer and hightail it back to Quan Loi. My passenger got out and the next thing I saw was a big flash of white light and a massive KABOOM! My back hit the back of my seat (the firewall on an H-13), and the next thing I knew I was engulfed in flames. I unstrapped my harness and exited the aircraft. I tripped over the left skid (you fly the H-13 from the left side) that obviously was splayed out by the explosion. As I picked myself up, I saw tracers flying everywhere and more flashes of light and big explosions everywhere. I worked (more like stumbled) my way to the artillery pits and away from the source of firing. I flung myself and the front and back chicken plate I was wearing [upper body armor helicopter pilots wore] over the sand bag parapet and landed in a heap in a big pile of 105 shell casings. A bare-chested artillery type grabbed me and asked if I was alright. I still had my helmet on and could hardly hear him over the din of the incoming fire.

I just made it from my exploded and now flaming helicopter to the artillery pits just west of the southern end of the airstrip. Incoming tracers were everywhere, as well as these constant big explosions. I peered over the sandbag parapet and saw my helicopter in a crumpled, mangled mess and burning furiously. The tracers were getting more intense as well as the big explosions.

As my head cleared, it was quite obvious that a lot of shooting was coming at us from the rubber trees on the east side of the airstrip. In the confusion, I saw artillerymen scrambling in the five-gun battery and then I kept hearing the screamed words "Beehive Rounds" [a shotgun-like projectile with hundreds of pencil eraser-sized, solid steel projectiles]. I moved over to hide myself behind the breach of the closest gun and watched the arty guys crank the barrel of the gun almost chest level. Other guys were carrying ammo from the cubby holes made of sand bags from the inside of the parapet walls. It was getting light now, and I could start to assess the situation.

The bad guys were all on line on the east side of the airstrip, firing from inside the rubber trees. Not only were we receiving automatic weapons fire, we were also on the receiving end of heavy mortar and RPG [rocket-propelled grenade] fire as well. All this was coming from the rubber trees, less than one hundred meters to our east. By now the 105 howitzers were all pointed at the rubber, and the barrels were at minimum elevation and I found myself in the bucket brigade of artillerymen carrying ammo from the cubby holes to the now rapidly-firing guns. Although I was a young, nineteen-year-old ex-high school football player, and still in pretty good shape, I started to notice how hard I was breathing and noted I was soaking wet. The sixty-pound chicken plate I was wearing didn't help either. Within a few minutes of constant firing, the incoming all but stopped. Dawn had broken and all you could hear now was the screams of the enemy wounded in the rubber plantation across the airstrip.

There was a large RF-PF (regional, popular forces—a Vietnamese version of a local militia) earthen fort between the artillery pits and the Special Forces compound on the west side of the strip. This was supposedly manned with two hundred RF-PFs. Like the ARVN, the RF-PFs liked to keep their families with them everywhere. During the heat of the action on the south of the runway, the RF-PFs abandoned their weapons and fighting positions within the compound and hightailed it into the rubber plantation to the west of the compound. The enemy (by now it was very obvious that these guys were NVA) moved across the middle of the runway en mass and took over the newly abandoned RF-PFs compound. Now we had friendlies (us) in the artillery battery and the Special Forces compound, with the NVA occupying the RF-PF compound between us.

The artillery battery commander called to move two 105 howitzers up to the RF-PF compound. The NVA were now shooting at us (and the Special Forces compound) from the fighting positions dug into the sides (little caves that opened to the inside of the compound) of the earthen RF-PF fortification. Once in position inside the RF-PF perimeter, the two howitzers fired the bee-hive armed guns directly into the entrances of the fighting positions. One by one, they cleaned out the bad guys.

It was now full dawn and everything had settled down. I went over to what was left of my helicopter. Obviously I was hit on the right side of the engine basket with an RPG. Except for the armor on the bottom and the back of the seat and the erector set tail boom, there was basically nothing left. I had already called for another aircraft, as I was now tasked to assist my Infantry Battalion on an insertion west of Loc Ninh. Nighthawk 6 [helicopter unit commander] was bringing me a new helicopter. I got a chance to view the carnage the bee-hive rounds did earlier. There were NVA bodies everywhere; all sporting NVA olive drab uniforms, pith helmets and brand new AK47s and RPG-7s. You had to watch where you walked because there were a number of dud Chicom 60mm mortar rounds sticking out of the ground.

It was close to ten when Nighthawk 6 came with my replacement aircraft. He rode back to Lai Khe on a Medevac. Surprisingly, we didn't suffer that many casualties. There were a couple of guys hit with shrapnel and another bunch with skinned knees and other superficial stuff that only required local patching up. The Battalion Operations officer (who spent most of his visit in the artillery battery), finished his briefing at the Special Forces compound and wanted me to fly him a few clicks west of Loc Ninh to a clearing next to the rubber plantation we were in.

The thick rubber trees of the plantation ended abruptly in rolling hills of grass and scrub. This was Montagnard [one of Vietnam's indigenous tribal groups] country due to the slash and burn agriculture and the scattering of little grass huts on stilts placed randomly over the rolling hillsides. We picked out an LZ for a Battalion-sized assault/insertion and called in the coordinates. We orbited to the west (right up against the Cambodian border) while the artillery prepped the LZ. Soon after that, the sky darkened by a wave of helicopters car-rying the Battalion. Before the slicks arrived, the helicopter gunships hosed down the tree line with guns, cannon and rockets into the rubber trees on the east side of the LZ. I popped smoke to mark the spot for the lead ship to land. The insertion into the cold LZ went as planned. The infantrymen started to go on line and head into the rubber.

Standard SOP dictated that I scout ahead of the Infantry. Mature rubber trees are as bad as triple canopy jungle to see into. I did the best I could and worked my way ahead of the advancing infantry to a grassy clearing and draw that sloped north, 500 meters ahead of the infantry. Scouting over the draw, it became very evident that a large number of folks moved through the grass based on the multiple trails leading into the rubber where the Infantry was advancing. No sooner did I radio my report to the Infantry ground commander than the friendlies came under heavy and wide-spread automatic weapons fire. Immediately artillery blocking fire was called in to impact to the south and west of the Infantry now in contact. I orbited to the north and watched the tree line to see if any of the enemy were attempting to flee to the north.

Sure enough I saw movement and then started to receive small arms fire from the tree line. We then called for additional artillery blocking fire to the north (left flank) of the friendlies hoping to force the enemy elements out into the open, grassy draw. When an Infantry ground unit gets into contact, things get pretty busy. Command and Control aircraft start orbiting high above. Artillery, helicopter gunships and Tactical Air usually support. I was on the bottom of the ladder trying to stay out of the gun-target lines of all this and still support the Infantry. I was tuning my single FM radio constantly, talking to the ground unit, artillery, gunship leads and hopefully, the Air Force FAC (forward air controller) who's on the scene. Out of the radio chatter a call sign I never heard before contacted the Infantry ground commander calling inbound from the south with 6 aircraft. I looked to the south, after calling a halt to the southern flank blocking fire, and saw six black aircraft approaching. I marked the south end and north end of the treeline (where the small arms was coming from) and then noticed that the incoming aircraft were Army Mohawks (OV-something). These are mid-wing, twin turbine prop-powered, with triple tail fins usually used for reconnaissance. I orbited to the west to stay out of everyone's way and watched the Mohawks make their run. These guys had wall-to-wall 2.75-inch rockets and pounded the treeline. They made three or four passes. It seemed like they never ran out of rockets. They snuffed out my smoke and disappeared. (Note: I never saw an armed Mohawk before and never saw one again.)

We had blocking fire to the north and south. The Infantry was pinching the enemy east into the grassy, rolling clearing to the east and north. I was orbiting over the clear area looking for Charlie to show his face (with the battery of 105s at Loc Ninh primed and ready). Without me knowing it, a large group of NVA were already in the clearing well to the north of me where the down slope of the draw of the clearing faced north. We didn't think they were that far north, but it didn't take long for us to put the Loc Ninh artillery on to the target. NVA were running everywhere. This was my first time of ever seeing live NVA up close. The artillery killed and wounded a few, and the rest moved back into the rubber trees to the west. I saw one guy that carried what looked like a big map case. He didn't appear to be carrying a weapon. I put my M60 on him and started shooting. He zig-zagged to avoid my fire and crouched down in the high grass. I hovered over to where I thought I last spotted him, which was right next to one of those Montagnard grass huts. He was gone. By now the Infantry was advancing, and the commander wanted that guy with the map case. I hosed down the area around the hut and the hut itself. Nothing! He was gone. Thinking perhaps he crawled into the hut, I hovered up close and looked in the opening (with the M60 pointed directly out front). I fired off a couple of bursts directly into the hut hoping it would open up the grass doorway enough so we could see in.

Frustrated, I said "the hell with it" and hovered right up to the hut and stuck my left skid into the thatch at the peak of the roof. The roof was perhaps twelve feet long. I figured I'd just pull the roof off the hut with my skids and then we could see inside. I started applying pitch and a little forward cyclic. Nothing!! The thing wouldn't budge. I didn't like being in such a hot area doing Montagnard home remodeling as I'd make an easy, stationary target. I pulled in even more power. The roof started to move but wouldn't come off. I tried to back out but discovered I was stuck to the damn roof. My left skid must have tangled with something. I was stuck hard. I added even more power and more forward collective. I was starting to panic (in the back of my mind I was already trying to figure out what to tell my boss and accident investigation board how I wrecked my helicopter with a grass shack attached). This was it. I was committed . . . I steadied the aircraft, applied more pitch and forward cyclic. I looked at the manifold pressure and boost (H-13-S Models were turbocharged), which were both pegged. Now the RPM started to bleed. I was at the point of no return. Just then, when I was about to give up, the roof parted. I was so scared, I never even looked if the now roofless hut had any inhabitants. I told the Infantry ground people I was heading back to Quan Loi to refuel and re-arm (I was just about out of gas anyway). Flying back to Quan Loi with half a Montagnard house attached must have looked kind of funny. With all the drag, I could only muster 40 knots. I called Quan Loi tower for landing. On final approach, the tower asked if I wanted to declare an emergency. I told them "no," and continued my approach to the 115-145 refueling pad on the south end of the runway. I shut down and looked at the carnage stuck to my left skid. By now there were lots of curious onlookers asking all kinds of questions about my supercargo. My passenger (the Battalion S-3) and I answered the questions as we worked trying to dislodge the roof from my left skid. Those huts must have been built to last a long time. They were all lashed together with twisted, multi-layered vines. It took a good twenty minutes, with the help of a fire axe the POL guy provided, to clear the wreckage. Refueled, rearmed and without the roof, we flew back and supported the Infantry for the rest of the day.

Charlie Company Commander Len Tavernetti after November 7

CAPTAIN TAVERNETTI WAS HIT FOUR SEPARATE TIMES (a bullet wound to his foot and multiple shrapnel wounds, primarily to his legs and lower torso) in his effort to organize and rally his troops. After the battle subsided and the relief force arrived, he was moved to the triage area and subsequently loaded onto a helicopter for a flight to the medical aid station at Quan Loi. There he was again placed in triage and put on a helicopter for the flight to the 24th evacuation hospital at Long Binh (near Saigon). He was placed in line for surgery and afterwards spent two weeks being stabilized for an aeromedical flight to Japan.

Just before Thanksgiving he arrived at the 106th General Hospital after a C-141 flight to Tachikawa and an ambulance ride to Yokohama. He had two more surgeries in Japan and then after fifty-nine days was returned to Vietnam. He was assigned to the 1st Brigade of the 101st Airborne Division in Phan Rang as a replacement. However, his wounds had not healed sufficiently, and he was again hospitalized for more operations in Nha Trang. The next day, January 31, the Tet Offensive began and the hospital came under attack. The patients lay on the floor with the mattresses on top of them during the attack. As the hospital filled, he was moved into a tent city nearby and then evacuated to Okinawa, where he remained for three weeks. He was then returned to Vietnam and assigned to the American Division in Chu Lai. He was placed on the G-3 staff in charge of the newly arriving units and the in-country training. In June his year in Vietnam concluded, and he returned to the states.

Len attended the Infantry Officers Career Course at Fort Benning and then was sent to graduate school in Tucson. He went back to Vietnam for a second tour in June of 1972, where he served with the 24th Corps in Da Nang on the G-1 staff working on the drug rehab center, PX, and mail issues. When he arrived in country there were 120,000 U.S. troops in Military Region I (the northern quarter of South VN). By the following June all of the divisions had departed, the corps was shut down, and Len's second tour came to an end as the major withdrawal of U.S. troops was being completed.

On returning to the states the army assigned him to the Engineer Topographic Laboratories at Fort Belvoir, Virginia, to work on new map designs as we entered the digital age. After four years he attended the Armed Forces Staff College in Norfolk and then was sent to the Airborne Test Board at Fort Bragg. His next assignment was with the U.S. Air Force at Wright Patterson AFB working on a new cargo plane that became the C-17. He finished his career on the DARCOM IG staff at Fort Belvoir.

He retired from the army in January 1985 and went to work with the McDonnell Douglas Corporation, which later became Boeing. He retired from his civilian career in February 2007.

D Company CO Ray Dobbins
The Rest of His Story

Wʜᴇɴ ɪɴᴛᴇʀᴠɪᴇᴡɪɴɢ Dᴇʟᴛᴀ Cᴏᴍᴘᴀɴʏ Cᴏᴍᴍᴀɴᴅᴇʀ Capt. Ray Dobbins about November 7, we continued by asking him about his experience after the battle. The story was quite compelling, and I'm sure that all who knew him would appreciate learning about it.

Captain Ray Dobbins recovered from his wounds, completed his tour, and rotated back to the states. He returned to Vietnam for a second tour in August of 1971. He was assigned to II Corps based in Pleiku in the Central Highlands. Dobbins would be an advisor to the 43rd Regimental Combat Team of the 22nd ARVN Infantry Division. The regiment was based near a small town called Tan Canh in Dak To Province, a largely mountainous area approximately ten to fifteen kilometers from the Cambodian border. The supply route between Tan Canh and the next closest large base at Kontum, thirty kilometers to the southeast, was closed at the time, and all supplies to the base had to be flown in by helicopter or fixed wing aircraft. When Dobbins arrived at Tan Canh there were between forty-two and forty-six American advisors for the forty-five-hundred-man regiment. Within a month, however, the American advisory team was cut to just two men, Captain Dobbins and Lt. Col. Sam Seeto. They had radio communications that could reach Pleiku, about forty miles to the southeast.

Captain Dobbins:

On November 7, 1971, four years to the day after Srok Rung, we were on an operation with two battalions of the regiment. Our night defensive perimeter was 15 to 20 kilometers from Tan Canh. We had been patrolling out of the NDP for about three days when we came under a mortar and artillery attack followed up with a ground assault. We had several direct hits on the bunker that I was in, but fortunately all they did was knock in some sand and debris on top of us. The NVA penetrated our perimeter and got to within 30 or 40 meters of our bunker, when we finally got them stopped and pushed them out of the compound. We had quite a number of casualties among our troops and we had several of their dead and wounded also. We got a medevac operation going and started removing our casualties, but every time a slick came in it drew mortar fire. It took the major part of the day before we were able to get our artillery fire accurate enough to take out the enemy mortars. The key factor there was when Colonel Seeto went up in a helicopter and was able to observe puffs of smoke from the enemy mortar tubes and direct the artillery on them.[9]

Captain Dobbins:

We had a lot of NVA activity in the region during that time, and by February–March we were literally under siege at Tan Canh. We were receiving 20–30 rounds of 122mm rockets every day. Also, the NVA were firing wire-guided missiles at us, and they were knocking out some of the South Vietnamese helicopter gunships that were supporting the base. The American units had been pulled out of our area by this point in the war. We had trained the Vietnamese and turned over our helicopters to them. So we had limited air support because of those missiles. The South Vietnamese helicopter pilots were very reluctant to fly with the threat of those wire-guided missiles, and fixed wing aircraft were taking a great risk to land at the base also.

In April we received intelligence reports that the North Vietnamese were moving large numbers of tanks and artillery pieces down the Ho Chi Minh trail. In order to beef up our forces in the area, division brought in another regiment, the 41st, to an abandoned base called Dak To airstrip which was about two kilometers from Tan Canh. Colonel Brownlee and Captain Cardin were the American advisors for the 41st regiment. A few days prior to this Colonel Seeto was replaced by Captain Kenneth Yonan, a West Pointer. I told him that if we should get attacked with rockets or mortars he should take up a position in the base's water tower. It was at the center of our compound and had a commanding view of the whole base area. He was to be early warning for the regiment if we had a ground assault, but if we started receiving direct fire he should get out of there because he would be a target if he remained in the tower.

On April 23, 1972, the NVA started heavy bombardment of Tan Canh with 122mm and 130mm rocket fire. They were even using delay fuses on some that would dig a sizeable crater wherever they hit. To our advantage they were firing them so fast that they were forgetting to arm them or the fuses were bad because many of them failed to go off. As I was running to my bunker I had a couple of them hit right next to me and it was kind of like an earthquake. They knocked me off my feet and I would tumble to the ground, but I'd get up and notice that everything was working, so I would resume running to the bunker. What was happening was that the rockets were impacting with those delay fuses plunging into the ground but failing to explode. I believe it was the intervention of God [Dobbins's mother was in daily prayer over her son]. At that time there was no aircraft coming in or going out, and it was that way for the next two or three days.

---

9. The attack on the unit outside of Tan Canh underscored the changing nature of the enemy threat in the area. Offensive operations gave way to a more defensive posture.

On the night of the 24th the Ben Het Special Forces base was overrun (about ten kilometers to the south) by enemy tanks, and they said that they were headed up toward us. There was a (dirt) highway between us and them. Colonel Brownlee and Captain Cardin at Dak To were between Ben Het and us. We had a lot of aircraft and artillery working around us, but still the rockets were coming in heavy. It was constant with no letup. All unnecessary personnel were ordered to evacuate the base. A short time later the regiment at Dak To airstrip was overrun. Brownlee and Cardin were forced to evacuate on foot. Cardin made it, but Brownlee was listed as missing in action.

The next night we could hear tanks running all over outside the compound. You could hear them rumbling around out there all night long. We had gunships over the base engaging them, but they were unable, with the armaments they had, to knock them out. I called Captain Yonan and told him, "Get the hell out of the water tower, we've got problems here." He replied "Roger that sir," and that's the last word I ever heard from Ken Yonan.

The morning of the twenty-fifth we had enemy tanks all over the place and we just had two tanks, M48s. We also had two jeep mounted recoilless rifles. That was the extent of our anti-tank capability. We positioned the tanks by the front gate. About a half hour before daybreak everything went quiet. The enemy tankers had lined themselves into two columns outside the gate and shut their engines off. It was still and quiet. The command bunker that I was in was about 50 meters from the front gate. Just before daylight they cranked up every tank they had in that column. They turned their headlights on and rolled into our 4500-man base. When they came in the front gate many of our troops went out the opposite end of the base. No one offered any resistance against those tanks. Neither of our M48s fired a shot, and neither of the recoilless rifles were fired.

The NVA tanks came through the compound, and they lowered their main guns and were firing point blank at our buildings and bunkers, blowing them up. I was in the command bunker with the regimental command team. The base commander, a lieutenant colonel, grabbed me by the arm and said, "Come on." He moved a desk, and behind that desk was a trap door that was a tunnel opening. He took me into that tunnel, and it had observation ports built into it. I could look through those ports and see what was going on outside. All hell was breaking loose within the compound. They were killing ARVN (those that remained), and ARVN were killing them. By this time upper levels of command were bringing in jet aircraft. I had a radio and I was letting them know where I was and directed their strikes around me. I was talking directly to the pilots. Our bombers killed 56 tanks during that engagement, but that was only about a third of what they had. We stayed in that tunnel for what seemed like an eternity, but actually it was about noon when the North Vietnamese found the tunnel entrance, and they started running the tanks over our tunnel, crushing it. By the talk that was going on around me, I was afraid that the ARVN were going to surrender. I knew the language relatively well, and they were talking about surrender. I knew that there was no way that I was going to surrender.

We had to get out of there. We went out a rear exit, and the ARVN went toward the North Vietnamese to surrender and I went the opposite way. Right near our exit point were some livestock pens where the ARVN kept their animals that were part of their food supply—hogs, chickens, and goats. The hog pen was built up off the ground about two feet, so I slid under that pen and stayed there hidden in the hog droppings all the rest of that day. Nobody saw me dive under there. I had a canteen of water and my rice. I didn't think about eating anyway, and I had my radio so I was still calling in air strikes. Actually, they were on their own, but I was talking to them making sure they knew where I was, and I was just monitoring their strikes. I couldn't see much from my location, but I stayed under there until it got dark. I knew I had to get out of there and reach the jungle as fast as I could.

When the Tan Canh base was overrun both Ray Dobbins and Ken Yonan were listed as missing in action. Ray's mother was notified of his MIA status and she began to pray for her son's safety.

I waited until well after dark, so about 10 or 11 o'clock I crawled out, and I ran right into a couple of ARVN that had been hiding under the chicken coop. They were right next to me the whole time, and I didn't even know that they were there. It turned out that they were guys that I knew. We started out from that location and had not gotten 50 feet when an AC 130 gunship came in and started dropping flares over the base. So we crawled into a culvert that was right there where the road passed over a low area, and the three of us stayed in that culvert the rest of the night and the next day.

The second night I decided I was going to leave a little earlier. There were still tanks on the parade field still burning, and there was ammunition in them that was cooking off occasionally. No sane person would want to go near them, so that was the direction that we were going to make our escape. But first I was going to go check out the water tower and see if I could find out what happened to Captain Yonan. So we started out crawling and there was not a flare . . . there was not a moon. It was dark as pitch . . . it was perfect for us to make our exit. We crawled some distance and were right by a three-quarter ton truck when we heard someone walking down the road, and we could see that they had flashlights. So we jumped up under that truck, but my feet were hanging out the end of it. These three North Vietnamese came down the road there and shined the light on my feet. I couldn't catch what they were saying, but later the Vietnamese told me what they were saying: "Oh. A dead American. We'll pick up those boots on the way back." They didn't kick my feet or check us out or nothing. I had my .45 in my hand, and I was ready to give it up; I was not going to be taken prisoner. They were going to a meeting or they would have taken my boots right then. When they came back and found me gone, they had to have realized that that was "Icebox 33" that had been laying there. "Icebox 33" was my call sign, and they knew that I was somewhere within or around the base because they had been monitoring my radio transmissions, and they had to have been looking for me.

From there I crawled up to the water tower and searched all around that area. The water tower had been blown down. I found several bodies, but I never did find Captain Yonan. From that area we went immediately out to an area of the perim-

eter that had a mine field. It was our best chance to get out of the perimeter undetected. When the North Vietnamese came in through the front gate, the 22nd
Division commander had his ARVN troops march through the mine field and
made them explode mines. He had them march through in front of him so that he
could get out. I didn't know that until I got out there and started breaching that
mine field. I had taken my shirt off and tied it around my neck and started crawling through there. If you get close to a mine the hair on your arm will stand up
and you can feel that. I had started out when one of the guys that was with me
said "Sir, come over here." I went over with him and there was a clear path
through that mine field where the ARVN had gone through. There were dead
ARVN bodies laying everywhere. And there were a lot wounded that were still
alive. At that time I told them that we would take all the ones that we could with
us. The two men that were with me and I took 19 wounded ARVN and moved
out about a kilometer to a kilometer and-a-half outside the perimeter. It was dark,
but there was still a FAC (Forward Air Controller) flying over the area, and he
was talking to me. I couldn't see him, but I could hear him up there. We had
changed our radios over to the emergency air-ground frequency. The ARVN
didn't have that frequency so the NVA [with the captured radios] couldn't listen
in on our communications. Mr. Vann,[10] my superior, came on the radio and told
me they were sending in a slick for me. It was just beginning to get light. I told
him if he comes in from the north and breaks east he should avoid enemy fire. He
told me to pop smoke [throw a colored smoke grenade, used to disclose your
position to aircraft]. I said, "I ain't got no smoke." I told him the only thing we
could do was to take off clothing and wave it so if you see somebody waving
clothing, "That's us!" So that's what we did.

We were able to make visual contact with the helicopter and he came in, but I
knew that if I got on that slick there wouldn't be any more, so I sent out my
wounded ARVN on it. We loaded as many as we could. The slick lifted off, but
he took off in the wrong direction and he almost got shot down. I mean he was
taking all kinds of fire . . . started smoking and everything, and Vann said, "Ray
are you hit, has your slick been hit?" I told him "I'm not in that slick, sir. I told
you to send that slick out to the east and you sent him out the other way." Then
Vann, said, "Ray I'm sending in one more helicopter. You damn sure better be on
this next one, I'm not sending out any more." The second slick came in and set
down, and I got everybody that was left on it. The pilot took off in the direction
that I told him to, and we zipped out of there without any problem and flew into
Kontum [about thirty miles to the south].

In a letter that Ray's mother wrote to him after she got word that he had
been safely rescued she noted that in her praying she had received an assurance
in her spirit that Ray would be ok and she gave God the credit for answering her
prayers on his behalf.

As a result of the North Vietnamese offensive in the area most of the American
advisory teams that were working with ARVN units in the region north of Kon-

10. Retired Lt. Col. John Paul Vann, at this time working as a civilian, was senior American
advisor for the II Corps military region, which included the Central Highlands area.

tum were listed as missing in action. Kontum was the nearest large town to the south of Tan Canh and that's where most of the ARVN survivors showed up. In subsequent days Ray was involved with reorganizing the remnants of his regiment. About 400 of the original 4500-man regiment were put back together. During this time Captain Ken Yonan's West Point ring was purchased in the town of Kontum by intelligence agents who brought it in, thus providing some measure of closure for Ray. He had not escaped and was either killed or captured.

After overrunning Tan Canh, the North Vietnamese kept pushing south, coming right down the road. They had our two M48s leading their column, and I understand they were being driven by our drivers. When we got overrun a lot of the ARVN just deserted and joined the other side. The North Vietnamese tank column continued south toward Kontum. At that time we had equipped our helicopters with the TOW missile system and those tanks were taken out with helicopter fired TOW missiles and air strikes. Mr. Vann declared that we had successfully defended Kontum. He came up there and the local village chiefs and the honchos of the area, all Vietnamese of course, got together and had a big party. Instead of spending the night, about eleven o'clock he decided he was going to fly back to Pleiku. He and his pilot got in their little LOH and headed back. There was a mountain range between Kontum and Pleiku and the road back followed the valley between the two. The normal flight pattern was to follow the road back and to fly up and over those mountains. Enemy on the mountain tops could shoot down at aircraft failing to increase their altitude at that point. They took off and within a short period of time we got a radio call that they had crashed and that in the morning Charlie Cardin and I were to organize a search and rescue party and to go out and retrieve Mr. Vann and the pilot.

The next morning the rescue party located the crash site and retrieved the bodies of Vann and his pilot. The fearless warrior, John Paul Vann, was dead. Ray noted that there was no evidence of enemy fire and the helicopter crash was due to unknown causes. It was a tragic end to an amazing military career.[11]

Ray's second tour was at its end. He rotated out of country (August of '72) and came back to the states and went to Fort Monroe, Virginia. He stayed there in the Army ROTC scholarship department until August of '73 and then was assigned to the Command and Staff College at Fort Leavenworth, Kansas. He instructed there until '76 when he retired from the army after twenty-one years of service to his country.

---

11. I would direct any interested readers to the book by Neil Sheehan, *A Bright Shining Lie*, (New York: Modern Library, 2009). The book chronicles the career of Vann and is a must read for anyone who wants to fully understand the Vietnam War.

Bibliography

Cantigny First Division Foundation. *Blue Spaders: The 26th Infantry Regiment, 1917–1967.* Wheaton, Illinois: Cantigny First Division Foundation, 1996.

Hay, Lieutenant General John H. Jr. *Vietnam Studies: Tactical and Materiel Innovations.* Washington D.C.: Department of the Army, 1989.

Maraniss, David. *They Marched into Sunlight: War and Peace, Vietnam and America, October 1967.* New York: Simon and Schuster, 2003.

Sheehan, Neil. *A Bright Shining Lie: John Paul Vann and America in Vietnam.* New York: Modern Library, 2009.

Index

About the Author

TEVE SIMMS was drafted into the United States Army in February 1967, at
e age of twenty-one. After nine weeks of basic training and nine weeks of
vanced infantry training he was sent to Vietnam as a replacement in the First
fantry Division. He served first as a rifleman and then as a grenadier in the
th Infantry Regiment's Alpha Company. On November 7 he was on the relief
rce that rushed to the scene of the Srok Rung battlefield. Much of the Srok
ung story is based on his first hand experience. The process of locating and
terviewing participants of the battle covered a period of eight years after
ending his first Blue Spader reunion in Chicago in 2001. Steve enjoys read-
g nonfiction books and has a particular interest in biographies involving
merican history.

he author, Steve Simms, on left, consulting with Gen. Paul Gorman at one of the
nnual Blue Spader reunions.